FRIEND of
Best

NORM

Voices of Maui

Second Edition

.

CreateSpace, Charleston, SC
Printed in the United States of America by American workers
ISBN: 1-4392-5555-5
EAN-13: 9781439255551
Library of Congress Number: 2009909539

Voices of Maui

ED - KUPUNA	CLIFFORD - ADVISOR	MALIHINI - CONCIERGE	RUDY - ENTERTAINER
HOKULANI - KUMA	DAVID - MINISTER	THEO - INNOVATOR	WILLIE - PERFORMER
CHARLES - ACTIVIST	GEORGE - FARMER	ANGUS - LEGISLATOR	JO ANNE - LEGISLATOR
JIM - ART DEALER	ROSELLE - MOTHER	ELLE - ADVOCATE	NORM THE AUTHOR

Written and Photographed by
Norm Bezane

MEMORABLE VOICES

"To know Barack, you have to know Hawaii."—Michelle Obama.

"We thought we moved to Maui for the beauty. It turns out we moved here for the beautiful people."—Community Volunteer.

"People traveled thousands of miles; they've been sold a commercial image of Maui. By now you know that we are so much more than hula girls, swaying palms and sunsets. We look to the mountains and we look to the sea. You see so much more than you have ever seen before—Sales Director.

"These were "a handsome people, hospitable, friendly, cheerful living in a beautiful land."—Captain James Cook, circa late 1700s.

Hawaiians had "the appearance of destitution, degradation and barbarism among the chattering, and almost naked savages, whose heads and feet and much of their sunburnt swarthy skins, were bare was appalling. Can these be human beings? — Missionary Hiram Bingham, circa 1823.

"If you love Maui, you have a responsibility to learn as much as you can. Don't make Hawaiian culture parsley on the plate. Make it the meat and potatoes." — Minister.

"Thirty years ago, when people adapted. They wanted to surf, hang out. Now it's all business. 'How can I make money off this condo?' Today they have to have a big house and want Maui to be like California." — Basketmaker.

Hawaiians "want understanding of who we are and what we can become, and understanding of the injustices that have been done and continue to this day."—Advisor.

"Stopping development is like trying to blot out the sun. It is not an alternative."— Resident of Olowalu.

"I am not a Hawaiian according to law. This hurts me deeply. You are Native Hawaiian only if you have 50 percent Hawaiian blood; I do not."—Cultural Advisor.

"Some Hawaiians embrace aloha, some don't. Some like nothing better than to find an "American" who appreciates the culture, the aina and aloha. Others remain hostile to those they believe descended from people who took away their land and their kingdom."—The Author.

"Some 70 percent of Hawaiians know of the past injustices; 60 percent feel resentment; 25 to 30 percent really are upset; a quiet majority is not involved."—Cultural Practitioner.

"I had a hard time going to school. I had to stand in the corner. I didn't know what a light bulb was. We were scolded when we used Hawaiian words. It was very difficult to read an English book; I didn't understand the English."—Activist.

Many people today claim they were thrown out of my bar. But I actually only threw out six."—Bar Owner.

TABLE OF CONTENTS

ACKNOWLEDGEMENTS

TO: Sara, Foley and Conor Bezane, the joys of my life and my frequent companions in Paradise. And to Maui, for its unique ability to nurture its native born and to attract adventurous and remarkable people, including those willing to tell their stories and provide their perspectives and opinions freely and honestly.

Also to people like Malihini Keahi-Heath of the Ka'anapali Beach Hotel for her support, guidance and aloha, and again to Conor Bezane, a superb writer and copy editor.

To Jan Stone Vlasak, formerly of Maui now living in Nebraska, for help on the manuscript, Uli Kirkegaard, the Maui Tech Guru, for last minute computer support.

To Lahaina News, Publisher Joe Bradley for permission to publish the columns and able Editor Mark Vieth who usually catches my mistakes and is kind to the prose.

And especially to Sheldon Meyers in Chicago, the perceptive Harvard University grad, who over the years finally managed to help me find my true self.

Finally, with no connection between the two, our new dog, Kea Aloha, who loves to grab pencils but thankfully did not eat this manuscript for breakfast.

VOICES OF MAUI

*In Hawaiian tradition, a conch shell
heralds what is to come.*

VOICES

*Remarkable people speak out on the joys and challenges living in
the land of aloha.*

They come from New York and New Zealand, small towns in the
Midwest, from Tokyo and Toronto, Munich to Mexico City and virtually
everywhere in between.

Two million visitors a year to a place, according to a tourist slogan, "where the world comes to play." This is destination Maui, Hawaii U.S.A, a magical isle whose beauty is matched by the beautiful people who live here.

Yet the curious—and the not so curious—rarely get to know Hawaiians, the rich stew of immigrants they pass on the way to the beach or the "locals" born and schooled in paradise.

Thus, Voices of Maui, a compilation of profiles of a remarkable people, descendents of Polynesian warriors and kings and queens and sugar plantation workers as well as recent 21st century transplants who live, work and play on the greatest place on earth.

For those who visit and or frequently revisit this greatest place on earth... for those whose Hawaiian experience will not be complete without better understanding this isle's rich culture... for those who may be unaware of what Hawaiians have to teach us...for those curious about the clash of cultures between original settlers on the cherished land and those who recently have bought into a new lifestyle...or for those who simply enjoy good stories, this is a chance to listen to the Voices of Maui.

One might ask what qualifies me with no Hawaiian blood in my veins, at least only in spirit, not having grown up in paradise to write Voices of Maui. Visiting 27 times over 30 years for 60 weeks doesn't. nor being a permanent resident since 2001 does not appear to be a qualification. Yet there is an inquiring mind, a passion to appreciate and understand this unique culture and a willingness to listen and learn.

Newcomers are not easily accepted, particularly by people whose ancestors go way back to the days of amazing voyages from the South Sea Islands, especially Tahiti. The phrase, "what do you know, you haven't been here that long" is sometimes said, but more often thought even about those who have lived the life of Maui more than this writer.

This writer is still waiting to be invited to his first true Hawaiian ohana (family) luau and has not yet made it to the epitome enjoyed by so very few newcomers—the Hawaiian form of the kiss, nose to nose. But there have been a good many "Hawaiian hugs," nevertheless most appreciated.

For many years, Native Hawaiians (Kanaka Maoli) suffered by not being "allowed" to know about their culture, possibly one of the richest in the world. Hawaiian language was banned in schools. Hawaiians gave their offspring names like Ed and George (one time school teacher and cultural advocate Ed Lindsey Jr. and slack key guitarist and taro farmer George Kahumoku Jr., for example).

Parents dropped the long oral tradition of "talking story," teaching the young about their heritage and traditions. Children no longer learned to recite their genealogy that minimally covered hundreds of years. The longest memorized genealogies took hours and hours to recite, with the teller not permitted to stop until concluding.

Thus, many of today's generations of Hawaiians, those who still have the magical 50 percent Hawaiian blood that entitles them to acquire rarely available so-called Hawaiian Homelands, and those with lesser percentages do not know their culture. Fortunately a Hawaiian renaissance is underway. Young Hawaiians once again are learning.

This reporter asks questions but the story is told in the voices of those interviewed. Subjects are often quoted at length through the magic of the new digital tape recorder and conversation often transcribed to capture what was said, fully and accurately (the writer's scribbled notes are often undecipherable).

The columns in Lahaina News are not about me. Seldom if ever on these pages can one find the pronouns, "I" or "me." Occasionally, there is the phrase—by necessity—this columnist. Thus the ideas here are not mine. They are the ideas, concepts and stories of people who are the real experts on what this greatest place on earth is all about. In effect, these essays are authored by them, not this columnist.

It's presumptuous to say that young Hawaiians, even others, could learn anything from a guy who grew up in Oak Park, Ill, walked by Frank Lloyd Wright's studio on Chicago Avenue on the way to the Petersen's Ice Cream Parlor and lived across the street from where Ernest Hemingway grew up and lived. Nevertheless, the privilege of getting to know just a few Hawaiians fairly well and to hear their stories has been the journalistic experience of a lifetime.

Enough self indulgence. It is time to listen to the Voices of Maui and ask, "Who are these fascinating people?"

The minister and basket maker who can trace his ancestors back 900 years or the Grammy award winner who grows ancient taro on a North Shore farm?

The former police officer who at 74 turned activist to preserve the land or the expatriate who watched the old Hawaii Five O TV show while at work in Germany, tired of rainy weather, and pulled up stakes to resettle and open a highly successful art gallery on sunny Maui?

The protester who helped force the U.S. government to give back an island or the transplant who sailed here from California to create and run a canoe festival renowned throughout the Pacific?

People like the insurance broker from the Virgin Islands who stepped foot on the island, fell in love at first sight, moved here within three years and now represents 10,000 people on the County Council?

Who are these people—people whose culture is built on love of the land, people who couldn't resist moving here because they were blown away by island beauty?

What do Kanaka Maoli, Native Hawaiians who believe their kingdom was stolen from them by the U.S. want?

Is aloha a way of life and genuine or simply a tourist catch phrase designed to rev up a luau crowd?

What do locals think, how do they live and why do many struggle?

What is it like to live here and subsist here?

And finally, when it comes right down to it, what makes them so special?

This collection of essays and profiles gives voice to what this magical isle and its people are all about. These are the Voices of Maui, not always heard, but here for all to learn from and enjoy.

ABOUT THE AUTHOR

About 40 years ago, Norm Bezane, then 31, a former reporter for Business Week magazine in Chicago, starting a new career in public relations and a first marriage that is alive and well to this day, strode onto a Maui lawn where white-coated stewards were passing out local delicacies (pupus). Against a backdrop of lush mountains, he waded into the Pacific Ocean for the first time and fell in love, like so many others, with the island of Maui.

Later, he and his bride of as many years followed up on numerous return trips made over three decades to realize a life-long dream and set up permanent residency. Ever inquisitive, he didn't take long to put back his hat as a journalist to begin to write about the remarkable people who grew up on or migrated to what he is fond of calling "the greatest place on earth."

Bezane writes from a unique perspective. Growing up elsewhere, he had much to learn and still—in the humble manner of the rich Hawaiian culture—has much more to discover. Hence the column Beyond the Beach written for Lahaina News, a lively weekly, and "Voices of Maui," a compilation of the best of his essays written since 2006.

Bezane is also the author of "This Inventive Century: The Incredible Journey of Underwriters Laboratories.

Hawaiians
and
Their
Culture

ED LINDSEY

Retired Teacher

Maui more than a playground

New York, it was once said, has a million stories. Maui doesn't have a million, but we have a great many indeed that deserve telling to malihina (newcomers), to visitors who have come to love this place and even "locals" who may have lost touch with their heritage and the fabric of their community.

A good place to begin is with Lahaina-born Ed Lindsey, who was educated at King Kamehameha III Elementary School and the prestigious Kamehameha Schools and is widely regarded as a Kupuna, a respected elder and spiritual leader.

A retired schoolteacher, Lindsey is passionate about giving back to the land he loves. People need to work together for this island, he said.

"One of the lessons I have learned is that you will be remembered by what you have done in this life," he explained. "At your wake, (your survivors) will get 20 minutes to say what your life meant."

One of the many ways Lindsey gives back is by spearheading the restoration of an ancient Honokowai Valley village far above the last Sugar Cane Train stop on lands that are part of Ka'anapali Development Corp.'s Ka'anapali 2020 project. Six thousand Hawaiians once lived there, tending well-irrigated taro patches behind ancient stone walls still in place below giant rock formations.

Lindsey, wife Pua and Native plant specialist Rene Silva spend most of their Saturdays in the village clearing away invasive species and replacing them with Native plants with the help of hundreds of volunteers.

The solidly built man remembers when Lahaina was a typical plantation town of mom-and-pop shops serving local people. "Now what we have are cookie cutter shops going after local money," he lamented. "We had a stronger sense of community then and bonds of friendship. Today we have people rushing around stalled in traffic."

Lindsey's sorrow is that too many regard Maui as simply "a playground, a Disneyland" where newcomers don't meet local people. They come in and move away "like tumbleweeds."

"My goal," this inspiring leader said, "is to educate people so they know the preciousness and what makes Hawaii and Maui separate from the rest of this world, and we have something to offer during these turbulent years."

Two things Lindsey would especially like from malihina are more interest in discovering the richness of Hawaiian culture and more respect for Hawaiian values centered on the 'aina, or land. This includes the spiritual side as well as the Hawaiian heritage.

He noted that Hawaiians have always been quick to adjust to new styles of living. The monarchs supported the building of the first high school (then equivalent to college) west of the Mississippi, and Iolani Palace in Honolulu had telephones and electricity throughout before the White House.

One of the culture's most important philosophies revolves around pono (doing the right thing). Kupuna believe one of the most important right things, Lindsey said, "should be fighting for quality of life, and that will benefit everybody and not just somebody walking in here and making a ton of money and walking out. You do not take our abundant resources for your own personal gain."

Although he believes entrepreneurs are learning, "When you start digging away at the layers of this onion, you look at the bottom, you see dollar signs. Is it cost effective? How can we bump up profits? It is important to keep these local companies healthy—but not unbridled. It's a two-way street."

As with all good things, the privilege of listening to Ed Lindsey, as he sat on a wooden bench under a big shade tree, came to an end with much left unsaid. This soft-spoken man gives his own views willingly, but leaves the listener with the option of accepting them or not.

Lindsey had a couple of suggestions for those looking for ways to enter into the community. "Join a hula halau (hula school), join a nonprofit. There are lots of Hawaiian non-profits out there. That is how you extend yourself. You bring certain skills, whether you are a doctor, lawyer, a dentist, Indian chief, salesman."

"This is what you share, and this can be more fulfilling than staying with just birds of a feather. People need to work together for the betterment of this island. Yes, it's a long trip. But as the Chinese say, it starts with a single step."

September 14, 2006

ED LINDSEY

Passing to a new 'aina: his invaluable legacy lives on

Puanani Lindsey continues the legacy.

Nearly three years after this column was written, Ed Lindsey left this earth for the ultimate 'aina. Maybe Ed knew the end was near. His prophetic statements in the first column are repeated in the second, based on a return visit to Honokowai Valley soon before Voices of Maui went to press.

More than three years ago, Edwin (Ed) Robert Naleilehua Lindsey Jr., Kupuna (respected elder), retired school teacher, protector of the 'aina (land) and advocate for, and practitioner of, Hawaiian culture and values, sat down for an interview for the first "Beyond the Beach" column.

Nine months ago, Ed provided eloquent testimony on behalf of the West Maui Hospital and Medical Center before the State Health Planning and Development Agency, helping it gain unanimous approval. It is unclear whether Ed had cancer at the time, but typically he did not wear the fact that he had cancer on his sleeve.

Each anniversary year of "Beyond the Beach," thought was given (but never acted upon) to do another interview with Ed.

Alas, Ed, at 70, passed away June 24, far too prematurely for the hundreds he touched, including this writer.

"One of the lessons I have learned," Ed said in my one and only formal interview with him, "is that you will be remembered for what you have done in life. At your wake, your survivors will get 20 minutes to say what your life meant."

Twenty minutes would not begin to cover all that Ed achieved. And so his memorial celebration — filled with tributes and song — lasted at least 90 minutes, with much still left unsaid.

Among the achievements almost too long to list were spearheading or playing a leadership role in Maui Coastal Land Trust (to stabilize and restore cultural lands), Project Malama Honokowai Valley, Project Malama Uku-mehame, Project Malama Kaheawa-Hanaula, Hui O Waʻa Kaulua (building a double-hulled voyaging canoe), ʻOhana Coalition (political group) and the Kaanapali 2020 advisory/planning group.

In May, the Maui County Council recognized Ed as "a beloved Maui treasure." In a eulogy, he was also described as "a Hawaiian warrior." The pride and joy of this man of aloha, beyond his family, was the restoration of Honokowai Valley village far above the last Sugar Cane Train stop along Honoapiilani Highway.

Six-thousand Hawaiians lived there for centuries, tending well-irrigated taro patches (there was no "show me the water bill") amid stone walls still in place below a large cliff.

Today, Ed's work continues much like it always has. One recent Saturday, some 40 volunteers headed into the valley to carry on the job of clearing away invasive species and planting native flower and fauna.

Puanani Lindsey, Ed's wife of 45 years who worked alongside him in the valley, has continued where Ed left off. New volunteers began with a tour of the new plantings, with Pua telling stories about the medicinal value of each plant.

When fiery red ants attacked her bare legs, she simply walked over to a plant, squeezed juice from the leaves, and applied it to good effect to eliminate the pain. Edwin "Ekolu" Lindsey III, the pair's son, listened nearby, committed to a leadership role for the project in the years to come. He absorbed his mother's talk story so he could repeat it someday. Then it was his turn, strolling along with the visitors to explain the stone-walled taro patches.

Although the trip to the valley began early, work for quite a few of the volunteers didn't start until about 11:30 a.m., when a chain gang was formed to bring small chunks of tree trunks and branches up from a gully to the road, where they would be turned into wood chips for pickup and hauling away.

Veterans of the effort had been at work since 10 a.m., using chain saws to cut down trees, then sending their remains to a kind of chain gang.

The Honokowai project is not just about reforestation. It is also about providing a much-needed cultural experience — a way for those who work there, including Hawaiians who have not been in touch with their culture.

Pua often leads community groups up to the valley, a trip that generally yields new recruits. Participation is largely confined to locals. All residents need to do is show up, almost any Saturday at 9 a.m. at the train station.

Two volunteers, formerly of California, joined up after looking for a volunteer opportunity. They've worked in the valley every week all year.

A lady from India who lives in Germany, who also worked in the valley for a year, received a fond farewell. All were following the advice of Ed Lindsey himself, who noted in the column: "Join a hula halau (hula school), join a nonprofit. There are lots of Hawaiian non-profits out there. This is how you extend yourself.

You bring certain skills, whether you are a doctor, lawyer, a dentist, Indian chief, salesman. This is what you share, and this can be more fulfilling than staying with just birds of a feather (meaning the people you usually hang out with). People need to work together for the betterment of the island. Yes, it is a long trip, but as the Chinese say, its starts with a single step."

MALIHINI KEAHI-HEATH
DAVID KAPAKU

Flag flap goes to core of issues

When artist Anita Marci was asked to fashion a logo to promote the display of fireworks for this year's July 4th celebration in Lahaina, she decided instead to create a painting called "Celebration Integration." A photo in this newspaper has sparked dinnertime conversation in Hawaiian households.

Art can be provocative to the beholder and spur debate. And so it has been and bothered some Kanaka Maoli (Native Hawaiians).

Do Hawaiians or part Hawaiians wave the state flag proudly? Should the Hawaiian flag, symbolizing overthrow of the kingdom to some sovereignty advocates, be associated with American independence?

Does the flag represent dependence, not independence?

On King Kamehameha Day commemorating the birthday of the unifier of the Hawaiian Islands this columnist brought together the artist with two highly respected Hawaiians. Ka'anapali Beach Hotel Concierge Malihini Keahi-Heath's great, great grandfather was a feather gatherer for the Queen Keopulani, one of the wives of Kamehameha the Great. Kahu David Kapaku whose ancestors came here 900 years ago.

According to Kapaku, as well as a short film shown at the burial place of Kamehameha on Hawaii Island, today's state flag with Britain's Union Jack in the corner is identical (except for an extra stripe) to the flag that Kamehameha I approved as the official flag of the kingdom in the early 1800s. That flag was the successor to an older one featuring a kahili (royal standard) and paddles to represent Hawaiians' connection with the sea.

The first post-contact flag influenced by the arrival the British had the union jack surrounded by an all red field. There was a time when Hawaiians raised the British flag when the Brits were in port and the stars and stripes when the Americans were here. Each side became upset when they saw the flag of the other flying.

To placate both sides—perhaps as a smart political move—today's flag incorporating both the jack and stars and stripes—was approved by king as the official Hawaiian flag. Thus, it could be argued, this "Kamehameha flag" is worthy of respect by kanaka maoli and anyone else who has lived here for the last 150 years.

Kahu David Kapaku and Malihini Heath smile for the camera after a good discussion on the flag issue with artist Anita Marci (center).

Yet, when Malihini Keahi-Heath first saw a painting with parts of the American flag and a small Hawaiian flag in the middle, she was offended. If it was the other way around, with the big flag Hawaiian and the American little, she said "maybe I would have thought differently.

"This painting is controversial," Kapaku declared, "because of the issue of statehood. The Hawaiian flag can be considered a symbol of colonialism by hardnosed members of the sovereignty movement."

Kapaku points out that the Apology Bill (see full description in the final section of this book) passed by Congress and signed by President Clinton officially apologizes to the Hawaiian people for the illegal overthrow of its government.

"If someone stole your car, it was taken illegally. But don't you still actually own the car? You look at this painting and you are going to see people disagreeing with the fact that we are part of the U.S. By this logic, 'stolen' Hawaii does not belong to the United States."

Most of the flag discussion focused on Hawaiians' loss of land, the core value of Hawaiian life for centuries and still the subject of reverence.

"We Hawaiians are considered a minority here," Keahi-Heath declared. "Our issues are huge." Hawaiians had paperwork showing they owned certain land for decades, if not centuries," she explained. Yet under Hawaii law, if land is unoccupied it can be claimed by any one who declares it as his own and pays overdue taxes.

Some of the land "owned" by the island's largest corporations was secured through adverse possession. Sugar growers grabbed water rights. Hawaiians whose lives were dominated by crops to sustain them left lands because streams dried up and they could no longer grow anything.

Leaving the land made it vulnerable to takeover. Growers, according to Keahi-Heath, abused the land, then decided, after a period of years, to abandon it, discontinuing crops and growing them elsewhere. "They abused the land so harshly, we can't go back and grow what we used to grow," she commented.

"Our land issues," Keahi-Heath added, "are even fought in court on another island," transferred there to discourage testimony of Maui people who would have to travel off island on short notice.

On land that we once owned, "we sometimes get challenged that we are trespassing. This is what hurts. Others have dominion over part of the land that once belonged to our ancestors."

Despite these differences," Keahi-Heath stressed, "we respect the Hawaiian flag. But the "little Hawaiian flag in the artwork is a symbol of our turmoil. For generations, we have been trying to be heard."

Artist Marci, who has put the painting up for sale, said she wanted the work "to be a symbol of peace and unity. I wanted to bring the two flags together like a floating island as part of a bigger whole."

Summing up, Kapaku said, "When I see the smaller Hawaiian flag, it makes me feel other people are still in charge of my destiny. Everybody has been deciding the destiny of the Hawaiian, but not the Hawaiians."

"We are called the host cultural but we have not hosted anything since 1893. What are we hosting when we are not the dominant culture? For me, it feels like I am being imprisoned within the borders of the U.S. Everything I believe in as a Hawaiian is being stripped. My space is getting smaller because everything is being stripped of me. That box (of the Hawaiian flag) makes me feel very claustrophobic."

If art promotes discussion and debate, so be it. On an island peopled by full-blooded Hawaiians, Portuguese/ Hawaiians, Japanese/Hawaiians, hapas and new arrivals we all gain by lending a sympathetic ear to the voices of this land's Kanaka Maoli. If, that is, we would only listen.

July 23, 2009

"aloha a Hui Hou, malama
Kou Kino — malama pono

aloha Nou!!

Malihini

MALIHINI KEAHI-HEATH
Concierge/Dancer

Bringing the spirit of aloha alive

Malihini—Hawaiian for newcomer to the land—has an apt name.
Concierge extraordinaire at what is properly billed as the most Hawaiian hotel, Malihini Keahi-Heath brings the spirit of aloha alive to other na malihini: first-time and longtime visitors to the Ka'anapali Beach Hotel (KBH). When she is not helping or educating guests, she is dancing hula for them almost every night on the Tiki Bar stage.

Named after an area in Moloka'i (her grandfather was a Kupuna, or spiritual leader there), Malihini is descended from a great-grandfather who came here from Tahiti in 1708. Her eight brothers and sisters have led a different life than their parents.

Malihini's dad, a fisherman known as "Uncle Moon," worked for many years for Pioneer Mill, planting and harvesting cane starting at 6 a.m., running heavy equipment and eventually moving up to supervisor. Off at 2:30 p.m., he'd take a break, have an early dinner, and be off to Napili Kai Beach Resort to perform as a musician until 10 p.m. on many nights.

Mom, known as Auntie Primrose, had a florist shop in Lahaina and used to buy turtles and filet them in her back yard. Three of her eight brothers and sisters, including a musician, are involved in the visitor industry. Her five children include a hotel engineer, waiter, and dispatcher. Her new husband of seven years, "Bonz," is a chef. Since he is from Massachusetts, she calls him "her missionary."

Malihini surfed and fished as a keiki (child), took up hula at seven, performed on a stage for the first time at 12, graduated from Lahainaluna High School, and soon was on her way to a long career in the tourist industry.

Starting in 1993, she served in a variety of posts at KBH before becoming a full-time concierge. Suggesting tours, answering guests' questions and making dinner reservations. Malihini often comes from behind her concierge desk to teach hula on the lawn three days a week. She also hosts a tour of the property in which she explains the medicinal value of various native plants.

Before there was a Ka'anapali Beach Resort, Malihini described Lahaina affectionately as being "nice." Everywhere you went there were familiar faces. When a child was born to that village, everyone was responsible for that child until they grew up. If you got out of hand, because you are on island, your parents knew it even before you got home," she said.

"We were taught to respect everyone of every age." She laments that parents today are not teaching this value. When she sees young people doing something wrong, Malihini turns feisty, getting out of her car to scold kids for not doing the right thing, or asking people to pick up trash they have heedlessly discarded.

One of her biggest passions is hula. She regards it as one of the few things of the past that "we Hawaiians have to hang on to." Learning the words and gestures is incredibly hard, even the first verse, she explained. And then there are six verses.

Malihini is also admired by her KBH colleagues for her remarkable ability to remember the names of previous guests. Her close relationship with them as they return year after year is seen every day as she "welcomes them home."

April 24, 2008

PART 1

HINANO RODRIGUES
Cultural Historian/Teacher

Preserving Maui: a Hawaiian responds

Hinano is my teacher. And as he puts it to students of his Hawaiian language and second culture class at Maui Community College's new West Side Education Center in Lahaina, "you will always be my student." If you spend 20 minutes a day, seven days a week, during the course and haven't learned Hawaiian, he said he will tutor you later for free.

What one is humbled by is how complex and how different Hawaiian cultural values are from western values. For this writer and most readers committed to being enriched by the experience, this shapes up as an endless journey of discovery, given its many nuances, with no end in sight.

Hinano Rodrigues—three-eighths Hawaiian, three-eighths Japanese, and two-eighths Portuguese, raised as a Hawaiian—is descended from great, great, great, great grandfather Kamakakehau, who was summoned by King Kamehameha I to Ukumehame to serve as konohiki (head overseer) of the King's cattle.

When he was one day old, Hinano joined the traditional Hawaiian system of hanai and was sent off for his first five years to be brought up by his grandmother, Louise Leialoha Kaahui, to learn Hawaiian ways. And every weekday, his real mother, Adeline Kumaileolihau Kaahui-Rodrigues, would journey from Wailuku to the new "dream city" of Kahului to visit him.

In this manner, the strong 'ohana (family) bonds that Hawaiians live by were created with young Hinano tied closely to his grandmother (really a second mother) for life. Through daily contact between birth mother, son and surrogate mother, the three generations formed a never-to-be-broken bond.

After schooling at Wailuku Elementary and Iao Intermediate, Rodrigues was off to Honolulu and Kamehameha Schools and the University of Hawaii. Sophomore year in high school, Hinano had—like a number of others—an epiphany after reading "The Queen's Story," the autobiography of Queen Lili'uokalani and her account of her overthrow by the U.S. government. Right then, Hinano decided to learn much more about Hawaiian culture.

Only 2,000 people across the islands, most over 65, could speak Hawaiian when his learning started. The language was dying, Hinano said. So he took two years of high school Hawaiian and four years in college (one of only three in his senior school class to study the language).

Back on Maui in 1975, Hinano became the first teacher of Hawaiian at Maui Community College. After a 20-year detour to California to get a law degree—his second epiphany was that law might be the answer to overturning court decisions that trampled Hawaiians' rights to land—Hinano was called back home in 2005 to keep a series of family promises after a Mainland career in state government and the private sector.

The Olowalu Lanakila Hawaiian Protestant Church chapel had burned to the ground in 1930. Sugar planters cut off water at his ancestral home's taro patch in Ukumehame in 1945 and the plants withered and lay dormant for 50 years. Hinano and his parents set to work. Today, water flows, the taro is growing and plans to rebuild the chapel are underway.

This is an activity for weekends. Monday to Friday, Hinano works as the only cultural historian on Maui for the state Department of Land and Natural Resources. Monday and Tuesday evenings, this dedicated cultural specialist teaches language and history courses at the new MCC on the Lahaina side of Cannery Mall. Wednesday nights are reserved for the General Plan Advisory Committee (GPAC), on which Hinano is a key member.

Truly a son of the land, Hinano has much to say about development, especially since his ancestral home sits amid what would be a planned new town in Olowalu.

"Stopping development is like trying to blot out the sun. It is not an alternative. It is not going to happen. We live in a capitalistic world. Capitalism snowballs. You cannot stop it. What we need to do is to have controlled development. We need to find a balance. This is a hard thing to do."

"Standing on the road and holding a sign is not a solution. The other side gets everything they wanted and you get nothing you wanted. And the development will go through. Say that a Hawaiian wants to stop development. Where does her husband work? He works for a construction company. No development will mean he will lose his job," he continued.

"It used to be that a developer would say, 'This is what I am going to do.' Now, it is turned around. We say, 'So this is what you want to do.' Now it is both sides coming together. I truly believe we should permit development only when developers can prove that they have water. Water is a limited resource."

As valuable as his insights on development may be, even more valuable is what he teaches about five great Hawaiian values. What are they? Many things Hawaiian, anyone who lives here. As Hawaiians say, a hui hoe, until later we meet again.

August 2, 2007

PART 2

HINANO RODRIGUES
Cultural Historian

Live aloha, embrace pono and much more

The beach is special. Green mountainsides and beautiful lands are special. Birds singing at dusk and flowering trees blooming are special. For those who choose to look—locals and visitors —there are those that are more special: Hawaiians, sometimes called Native Hawaiians, perhaps more accurately described as Kanaka Maoli.

These special people, according to Cultural Historian Hinano Rodrigues, believe in these five things:

Aloha. Aloha is not simply a greeting for hello or good morning. Aloha is compassion. Aloha comes from within, a belief that every person deserves to be treated fairly, honestly and with sensitivity all the time. Aloha is pronounced with quick flourish. It is not, as so many entertainers and presiders at meetings proclaim: aloooo—ha. Aloha, mispronounced, degrades its meaning.

Mana. Hawaiian ali'i (kings) had more *mana* than anyone else. Upon death, their *mana* remained in their bones.

Ali'i were buried in secret places so no one could dig up the bones and acquire their *mana*.

Today, these bones can appear almost anywhere soil is turned and their presence is one of the reasons Hinano and the State Historic Preservation Agency is required to make decisions at least 20 times a year on Maui to decide whether bones found inadvertently—Native or non-Native and more than 50 years old—can be moved or stay in place and what, if anything, can be built over them.

Mana is power. *Mana* is the power within to create positive change. Every *ali'i*, every Hawaiian, every one who lives here or visits, has *mana* to one degree or another. The challenge is to put *mana* to good use. *Mana* is the power to set the tone of relationships.

Mana can also be regarded as charisma, something people say President Jack Kennedy had and what KPOA radio star Alaka'i Paleka has in abundance. Name your charismatic character. One example of *mana*: your willingness to smile at someone. Check the reaction.

Niele, meaning you are too inquisitive. Hawaiians abhor the idea of asking questions just as husbands who are lost in their cars do. Even today, some think the reasons those brought up here don't ask questions at meetings is because of *niele*. Hawaiian inquisitiveness involves learning by observing, not asking.

Maha'oi, meaning intrusiveness. Hawaiians ask permission for everything they do. Can I pick mangoes from your tree on Saturday? A Hawaiian's usual generous response is "sure." But do not assume permission is endless. Want to pick mangoes next Saturday? Ask again. Or better yet, Hinano jokes, "plant your own tree."

Pono, or balance. Live your life with balance, with moderation. When things are out of balance, put them back in balance. For this to be column *pono*, more has to be said. There is no one Hawaiian and no single stereotype.

Some Hawaiians embrace aloha, some don't. Some like nothing better than to find an "American" who appreciates the culture, the aina and aloha. Others remain hostile to those they believe descended from people who took away their land and their kingdom. A few do authentic, traditional hula, most don't.

Hawaiians, we are reminded, are doctors, lawyers, legislators, entertainers, cooks and auto mechanics. And some Hawaiians are in jail, all too many alienated, discouraged and distraught.

The best we can all do is to seek understanding, embrace some of the values, and try a little harder to live aloha and strive to be *pono*.

August 16, 2007

JAMIE DEBRUNNER
Sales Director

Maui is more than hula girls, palms and sunsets

Just about a year ago, Old Lahaina Luau's Jamie DeBrunner had a vision. Since visitors often asked questions about Hawaiian culture that dancers and waiters couldn't answer, why not give the staff training?

Thus was born *Ho'omana'o* (to remember), a three-hour treat in things Hawaiian offered to visitors, residents and school children three days a week at Moali'i, the oceanfront home of the luau.

Greeting visitors finishing a fine breakfast, the sales director and cofounder of the morning event explained that the goal of *Ho'oman'o* is to perpetuate Hawaiian culture. "There were a million *Kanaka Maoli* (Native Hawaiians) here when Captain Cook came. Now there are only 12,000 left," she said. "We want to remember the past so we can perpetuate it into the future."

Understanding, she noted, starts with language. She passed out a slim sheet of paper – a guide to pronouncing Hawaiian vowels and letters – and has her guests repeat Hawaiian words. "Very few," she declared, "will have the opportunity to learn and see what you experience this morning."

The crowd splits up into small groups to visit three Kulana stations. In the first, we learn about Laka, the goddess of hula, and the three forms of hula practiced from ancient to modern times. About a dozen musical instruments with difficult Hawaiian names are demonstrated and explained one by one.

"Hula," said "teacher" Paula Gamboa Gomez, "explains everything we see, hear, feel, and touch."

The 30-minute session ends with dads, moms and little kids picking an instrument of choice and playing as they dance some basic hula steps. Each was born to the task, and you did this for eternity," she explained.

In the next session, Native Hawaiian Tanya Marie Mailelani Ferreira, with a degree in Hawaiian Culture explored Hawaiian life and how every Hawaiian had a specialty, from fishing and farming to tapa making.

Summing up for visitors, she said, "People traveled thousands of miles and have been sold a commercial image of Hawaii. But now you know that we are so much more than hula girls and swaying palms and sunsets. We look to the mountains and we look to the sea. And you see so much more than you have ever seen before."

In session three, muscular Hawaiian "warriors" told tales of King Kamehameha, demonstrated weapons, and explained that ali'i fought and killed other ali'i, not for land but to acquire more mana.

Session three, like each session, ended too soon. Smiling guests headed for their cars, all much richer for the understanding they have acquired of Hawaiian culture.

"It was wonderful – better than the Polynesian Cultural Center," said one guest. "My kids will never forget it." Talking story afterwards, Jamie said, "This is a journey for us that has just started. I was told in school that I needed to learn Japanese to succeed in the tourist industry here. I should have learned Hawaiian. But it is different now."

We self studied for a year; we started off to teach ourselves and realized if we didn't use it we would lose it. We said, 'Let's share it with visitors.' We bring in fourth-graders from King Kamehameha III Elementary School who are studying Hawaiian culture and plan to bring in many, many more school groups.

Residents and visitors alike would do well to practice the phrase learned when we started the day: *E komo mai.* Come in.

October 26, 2006

KAHU DAVID KAPAKU
Minister/Basketmaker

When you fall in love, learn all that you can. "If you love Maui, you have a responsibility to learn as much as you can," declared Kahu David Kapaku.

Sitting in beautiful Honokohau Valley, where his direct relatives settled 900 years ago, Kapaku, a minister of the Ka'ahumanu Church and holder of bachelor's, master's and doctorate degrees in Religious Studies, has powerful stories to tell.

What this smart, perceptive son of the north shore has to say about change sweeping the island, development, Hawaiian traditions, Christianity and mythical gods offers anyone curious about this place much food for thought.

Hawaii has long been a magnet for newcomers, setting up a clash between new and old. When Tahitians migrated to the Big Island ten centuries ago and changed the religion, they enlisted thousands of Hawaiians to carry two million pounds of rocks 20 miles to build more elaborate *heiau* (places of worship) for human sacrifice.

The Makihous, the family name on his mother's side, wanted none of this and fled to Hana on Maui.

Later, they traveled far around the coast to the most beautiful spot they could find: Honokohau Valley. Kapaku's great, great, great grandfather fought with King Kamehameha I's warriors in the bloody battle of Iao Valley.

Chiefs, priests and taro farmers, all ancestors of Kapaku, thrived. Much later, Chinese immigrants came to their valley to help with pineapple. And then came resorts and people arriving on jet planes. Some of the newcomers assimilated, some didn't.

"There are people who have been here 40 years who still do not understand Hawaiians or our traditions," Kapaku observed. "Thirty years ago, when people came to live here, they adapted. People wanted to surf, just hang out. Now it is all business. 'How can I make money off this condo and sell it for twice as much.'

Today they have to have a big house and want Maui to be like California." "Yet there is still a Hawaii where you can hear the wind, you can hear the flowing water. This is what people imagine Hawaii to be. But some say, 'I need more money. I will put a house here. I will build another house there. I will LACE this whole area all the way to Olowalu. It's insanity," he said.

"People who first come here have a dream of what it would be like," he said. Visitors the minister meets are disappointed. "They say, 'I think Maui is beautiful,' but they have old pictures in their minds that Maui is a balmy place. They come and see a Costco, a Wal-Mart, and say they were not expecting that. This change is very disturbing. it's disappointing to see very expensive homes that no one is living in – $10 million, $15 million, and no one is there.

The greatest disappointment is to see the Hawaiian people having to leave because they can't afford to live here." I tell people, 'If you went to China, would you expect to see Chinese? If you come to Hawaii, would you expect to see Hawaiians?' Visitors are surprised to learn the percentage of Hawaiians on Maui is small. The typical reaction is, 'Are you kidding me?'

For Hawaiians, love of the land is paramount. This love is shared by many newcomers. "The first thing people see when they come here is the beauty. The unfortunate thing is, that is not all there is to see. When you fall in love, you want to know everything. And you begin to learn about (Hawaiians). You see a tree and it is beautiful. But there is more beauty under the surface if you could see the whole thing," he explained

October 26, 2006

PART 1

CHARLIE MAXWELL SN.
Activist

Marrying a smart girl makes the difference

Getting to know a Hawaiian is not always easy for the newcomer. At a recent community meeting, a good number of Hawaiians - but not all - protested in anger, as they believe the graves of their ancestors would be desecrated with construction of the new road. Whether this is true is unclear.

Earlier that day, by chance, this columnist met with Uncle Charlie Maxwell (Kahu Charles Kauluwehi Maxwell, Sr.) to do what Hawaiians have done for generations: exchange ideas (talk story is the popular phrase).

Before reviewing some of the issues, this cultural practitioner told a tale that sheds important light on what Hawaiians have faced that still shapes what they say and do today. Known like so many as "Uncle," because every Hawaiian is often considered to be related to every other Hawaiian, Maxwell led an early childhood less remarkable than it was typical.
The conversation is repeated here at length.

Now a Native Hawaiian activist, priest, spiritual advisor and self-described cultural practitioner, Maxwell was born on the Western tip of Maui in Napili 71 years ago. He went to school in the 1950s.

His great, great, great, great grandmother had rights to ancestral lands that stretched all the way from Iao Valley near present day Wailuku to the Ma'alaea isthmus that links two of Maui's dormant volcanoes. These lands have been long lost to descendants of missionaries.
(Incidentally, whether the influences of missionaries on Maui and the islands has been good or bad remains a topic of vigorous debate even today.)

Speaking Hawaiian at home, Maxwell lived in Kula on the slopes of Maui's great volcano Haleakala. There he found his early school years extremely challenging, to say the least.

"I had a hard time going to school," he said. "I had to stand in the corner. I didn't know what a light bulb was. We were scolded when we used Hawaiian words. It was very difficult to read an English book; I didn't understand the English."

Hearing the old rhyme, "Jack and Jill went up the hill to fetch a pail of water," Maxwell said he did not know what a pail or hill was, let alone fetch.

"I just read it; I didn't know what it meant. I knew it had to do something with *wai* (water)," he explained. Comprehension was zero. This is a problem with generations of Hawaiians. "We don't use English words at home - just broken English. My grades were so bad I became a clown (to endear himself to teachers).

"All the teachers liked me. Rebecca Raymond was my fifth grade teacher; she took special interest in me and I learned my times tables. After that, everybody ignored me and I forgot it all," he said.

When, he graduated from eighth grade, a teacher told him, "If I was you, I would marry a smart girl." And so he did. "I was spoiled. As soon as I got to 13, my father said, 'I am sending you to Lahainaluna (the first high school west of the Rocky Mountains founded by missionaries), because you are going to be a man.' For one year I cried," Maxwell recalled.

Freshman then underwent a kind of hazing. "Later, I wanted to do to the freshmen what they had done to me. I became *kolohe* (naughty). When I was a junior, I had 500 or 600 hours (of detention), so I quit school," he said.

Dropping out, he could easily have wound up like thousands of his Hawaiian brothers and sisters with lost self-esteem, who make up a large portion of today's prison population.

Instead he went to Baldwin High School and soon met the love of his life: a pretty 17-year-old who went on to become one of this island's leading *kumu hulas* (hula teachers). Luckily for Charles, she also happened to wind up class valedictorian.

Charles had met "the smart girl" he was told to find four years before. He recounts that his future wife, Nina, came up to him and said, "Oh, you are so luscious."

"That night, I went to a football game and found out she was a cheerleader. She waved. Her father knew my father well. By the time we finished our senior year, we were deeply in love," he said.

"So my father said, 'You want to marry that girl? Go ahead - you come live with me.' I had no job, nothing. Everybody said that it wouldn't last, and it lasted one month short of 50 years." (Charlotte Ann "Nina" Maxwell, once a lead dancer for the revered Emma Sharpe, passed away two years ago.)

"I went to work as a laborer, and one day the boss told me, 'you do not have to come back tomorrow." Thanks to an uncle, Maxwell was accepted by the Maui Police Department.

"Every case I was on the road, I would call my wife because I never knew how to spell or type. For three months she typed all my reports, and then she made a mistake. Then they made me correct one sentence and it took me two hours," Maxwell said. So his sergeant told him, "If you don't learn in three months you are out." So the smart girl taught him to type (at 100 words per minute.)

May 8, 2008

PART 2

CHARLIE MAXWELL SN.
Activist

Uncle's 35 year fight for Hawaiians

After reading "Hawaii's Story," Queen Lili'uokalani's vivid account of the overthrow of the Hawaiian Kingdom by U.S. armed forces in 1893, cultural practitioner and Kahu (Rev.) Charles Kauluwehi Maxwell Sr. of Pukalani had no doubt he should become an activist.

Hawaiians needed to fight to regain their lands and rededicate themselves to preserving their fast-disappearing culture of spirituality and aloha.

Since 1975, his quest for justice has brought Maxwell to Washington, D.C., and the White House, to sacred burial sites at Honokahua Bay and to the valleys of Kaho'olawe, where Hawaiians were once forbidden to enter.

In Washington, Maxwell pulled no punches with influential senators while explaining the need to recognize Native Hawaiian rights and protect ancient burial grounds.

Dressed in an aloha shirt while his colleagues wore suits, Maxwell told senators he doubted that many even knew Native Hawaiians existed. Frustrated with the conversation, as the *Kupuna* (elder) tells it, he stood up and pounded the table.

"You speak in a language that I don't understand. You are talking about my island," he said. "Everything went quiet. After that, I got invited to all kinds of places – the Oval Office (of the President) and the Rose Garden (at the White House)."

Testifying before Congress, Napili-born Maxwell told how revered iwi Kupuna, ancestral bones closely connected with Hawaiian spirituality, had been bulldozed and desecrated while preparing the original site of the Ritz-Carlton, Kapalua. Native Americans, present in full regalia, cried in sorrow and empathy when they heard his story.

In the end, Uncle Charlie and his colleagues played a key role in the passage of landmark federal legislation that put stringent procedures in place to protect the burial sites and artifacts of all Native Hawaiians and Native Americans.

In 1976, the 200th anniversary of the birth of American freedom, Maxwell decided to create a "national incident" to highlight injustices done to Native Hawaiians and assert their land rights by occupying Kaho'olawe Island.

Once an idyllic land opposite Ma'alaea, Kaho'olawe was filled with more than 2,000 cultural sites. Largely uninhabitable because of overgrazing, it was turned into a World War II practice bombing range shortly after Pearl Harbor.

Even in 1976, it was used and is still off-limits to everyone, despite a government promise to return it years before.

Tahitians, among the most prominent Polynesians populating these islands eons before, used Kaho'olawe as a reference point to and from Tahiti. (The western portion was called Lae O Kealaikahiki, meaning pointing the way to Tahiti.)

The island was regarded as special because it was an ideal departure point for voyages back to Tahiti – the North Star and currents pointing the way.

Maxwell handpicked Kanaka Maoli (Native Hawaiians) from every island for "an invasion." Nine, including Moloka'i activists Walter Ritte Jr. and Dr. Emmett Aluli (my recent colleague on the Maui County Health Care Task Force), made it to shore. Maxwell, who made a preparatory trip the previous fall, plied back and forth in a boat diverting the U.S. Coast Guard while the others landed.

The Kaho'olawe nine were eventually captured, arrested, and some served jail time. To make a very long story short, Kaho'olawe is now a protected preserve, no longer a bombing range. Only partially cleared of unexploded ordnance, it's scheduled to become sovereign Hawaiian territory apart from state or U.S. control.

Maxwell parted ways with the original activists and moved on to other things. Later, The Protect Kaho'olawe 'ohana was formed. The group now brings volunteers to the island every full moon to undertake the formidable work of restoration.

Maxwell's priorities over the next three decades were significant: heading the Hawaiian Advisory Committee of the U.S. Civil Rights Commission, chair of the newly created Maui/Lanai Islands Burial Council for many years, and serving as Kupuna to Haleakala National Park and the Maui County Council. But that is another story.

May 22, 2008

PART 3

CHARLIE MAXWELL SN.
Activist

Essence remains with the na iwi (bones)

Please Kokua (take care of) this ancient burial site by not stepping on the lawn is the message on this plaque placed near where iwi (bones) can befound by the hundreds.

In case you haven't noticed, Native Hawaiians and Americans are different. According to activist Charlie Kauluwehi Maxwell Sn., American culture is built upon materialism. Hawaiian culture emphasizes spirituality.

Your big responsibility if you live here, the Hawaiian storyteller and cultural practitioner believes, is to understand the place you call home. To Hawaiians, this is a spiritual place and the most basic cultural belief is Hawaiians' respect for the dead.

"Unlike Western society, Kanaka Maoli believe that part of their essence remains with the na iwi, the bones of the dead. And places of kana (burials) are sacred grounds.

In 1986, Maxwell got a call from then-Mayor Hannibal Tavares about iwi that had been located on the proposed site of the Ritz-Carlton, Kapalua on Honokuhua Bay. The man who was to become head of the Maui/Lana'i Islands Burial Council knew exactly what he had to do.

Construction crews had disturbed 800 graves, among 2,000 or more laid in layers on the site. Landowner Colin Cameron, according to Maxwell, insisted his hotel had to be built on the cliff on the edge of the bay filled with gravesites. Hawaiians said, in effect: no way.

Protests began. A vigil at Iolani Palace, former home of Hawaiian monarchs. Thirteen hours of negotiations between Hawaiian leaders, Cameron and then Gov. John Waihee. Cameron caved—but at a price. He agreed to move his hotel if the state paid $6-million ($10-million in today's dollars) to acquire land for a cultural preserve.

Ever since, Cameron has been variously praised for scrapping his design and relocating the hotel and vilified for fighting the change. Since then the hotel has partially made amends through its annual Celebration of the Arts cultural festival that fosters a community dialogue with Native Hawaiians.

According to the agreement, Maxwell and six others would be empowered to return 800 skeletal remains to the site, now a grassy field forbidden to walk upon without permission.

Honokuhua Bay, one of six that line the shores of West and Northwest Maui, remains a serene vista thanks to efforts to respect the sacred burialplace for hundreds of Kanaka Maoli interred their over the centuries. Ritz Carlton,Kapalua was re-sited after being redesigned and built well back of kai (ocean).

The iwi would be wrapped in kapa (also known as tapa cloth) especially prepared in the old way. Maxwell describes on his web site: "We started to wrap the remains. We would come… at eight at night and go home at three or four o'clock in the morning for three and a half months." On midnight of the last night, as Maxwell tells it, under lit torches, with a chant about to begin, a Hawaiian exclaimed: "Eh, ho'ailona" (An auspicious event.)

"We came to the edge of the cliff and when we looked down we barely saw the outline of one kohala (whale), the whale turning on its side and slapping the waters."

For 15 minutes, the whales slapped, and the Hawaiians cried. Owls (pueo) flew over, signaling the spirits were reunited with their iwi at Honokuhua. "Whoooo, whoooo, whoooo, they screamed and went right up to the mountain," Maxwell wrote.

"Everyone was dressed in the black malo (loin cloths)." Kahu Charles Maxwell Sn. said he was "privileged to be there." Hawaiians have an expression, a pledge to ancestors: La'iki keha 'O Kou moe lau (the dignity of your long sleep will be preserved.

The Hawaiian soul is in the bones where mana, their essence resides. Upon death, their *mana* remained in their bones. To Kanaka Maoli, their sanctity is to be defended at all costs. Sensitive issues like lack of respect for the iwi, the overthrow of the Hawaiian Kingdom, the concept of land ownership literally foreign to Hawaiians, and the seizing of lands still embitter many Hawaiians, according to Maxwell.

"About 70 percent of Hawaiians," he says, "know of these injustices; 60 percent feel resentment; 25 to 30 percent really are hung up on this and are upset at a quiet majority that is not involved.

There are at least 20 Hawaiian groups seeking address of grievances including those who want the U.S. to sanction a Hawaiian Nation within a Nation and the return of vast acreages. One of this year's clashes of cultures is the Lahaina Bypass, a short stretch of the proposed route would run over terraces that could—though not proven—include iwi.

There are no easy answers. Should the land serve the culture, the dead, or all three? Maxwell is philosophical, noting that Hawaiians need to move beyond bitterness and can make no progress unless they make the best of it.

Maxwell is here to give such advice, as he proudly points out on his web site, after a recent warning from doctors that he wouldn't live six months without slimming down from a very unhealthy 423 pounds. Now, thanks to a crash exercise program, a healthier Maxwell has lost 173 pounds and has become vigorous again. Maxwell has many stories to tell and even three columns offer only the highlights. Go to his site, moolelo.com, for more.

Postscript: Archeologists discovered no iwi on the site of the Bypass, allowing it to move forward).

BUMPY KANAHELE
Activist

A bumpy road to no one knows where

Bumpy Kanahele poses next to a photo of his favorite queen.

On the 116th anniversary of the 1893 overthrow of the Hawaiian Kingdom on Jan. 17, this columnist sat down with Pu'uhonua Dennis "Bumpy" Kanahele, identified on his website as the head of the "Hawaiian

Nation," to talk story about the complicated, sometimes confusing Hawaiian Sovereignty movement. Where is it going?

Bumpy, nicknamed that because of the frequency with which he bumped his head as a keiki (child), is just one of many Hawaiian activists. He heads one of several dozen Native Hawaiian groups with differing agendas, including restoring the Hawaiian Kingdom, creating sovereignty areas within the state, or reclaiming lands they believe were stolen in 1893.

Bumpy, among the most visible of activists, believes 2009-10 will be the years the long simmering issues come to a head.

Once called a hardcore militant by the Los Angeles Times, Bumpy in the 1980s led a move to occupy 300 acres of land on the east coast of Oahu at Makapuu Lighthouse. He fought for, and won, a fight to create Pu'uhonua 'O Waimanolo, a 45-acre site where Hawaiians were granted sovereignty by the estate.

In a tangle of efforts, the fervent Kanaka has been imprisoned 14 months for brandishing a shotgun during a confrontation with police on occupied land, and a second time elsewhere.

In 2002, Gov. Ben Cayetano pardoned him for both offenses. Now dividing his time between Maui and Oahu, 54-year-old Bumpy now says he has learned from experience and now takes a more moderate approach.

Kanahele's "Nation of Hawaii" wants to engage in a political process to sort everything out by holding a constitutional convention of Native Hawaiians. He now claims 3,500 signatures, including some gathered on a birthday celebration for Queen Lili'uokalani in Banyan Tree Park in Lahaina last year.

The petition emphasizes the right of the Native Hawaiian people to proclaim self-government under the United Nations charter. Delegates would be elected by voting district.

This initiative takes its inspiration from the so-called "Apology Bill," Public Law 103-105 (See Epilogue), signed by President Bill Clinton. The resolution states that "a small group of non-Hawaiian residents and citizens of the U.S. (in 1893 did) overthrow the indigenous and lawful Kingdom of Hawaii," and "Financiers deposed the Hawaiian monarch."

A fight over crown – or ceded – lands is also coming to a head. Crown lands are all lands originally owned by the monarchy and Hawaiian people. Ceded lands is a term for the same lands – 2.1 million acres Bumpy claims that were taken from the monarchy and controlled ("owned") by the territory and now the state.

A 2008 ruling by the Hawaii Supreme Court called a halt to the sale of all ceded or crown lands, prohibiting the state from selling, exchanging or transferring them. The state believes the decision by its own Supreme Court was deeply flawed and has appealed the ruling to the U.S. Supreme Court. A high court decision could come at any time.

If courts decide Hawaiians in fact own crown or ceded lands, the decision could mean that current "landowners" would need to negotiate with Hawaiians on a settlement. Current owners might be able to continue using the land they "own" by paying a leasing fee to the true owners.

All these messy questions relating to sovereignty and land could bring with them complicated situations with perhaps impossible or improbable solutions.

Making sense of this mess is a tall order, but one well worth pursuing for anyone who cares about Hawaii. Beyond the Beach plans to revisit this subject from time to time this year in humble pursuit of perspective that is hopefully useful. The batteries are fresh and the new digital recorder is ready to capture the views of anyone who wants to speak up.

February 5, 2009

CLIFFORD NAE'OLE
Cultural Advisor

Open the gate and come to the Ritz

Clifford Nae'ole like his ancestors wears no shoes

When the 15th annual Celebration of the Arts officially opens at the entrance to the Ritz-Carlton, Kapalua, Kanaka Maoli and resort Cultural Advisor Clifford Nae'ole will be near center stage. The festival planned by Nae'ole is a must-attend annual event for anyone who wants an introduction or continuing education in Hawaiian culture.

A spiritual sunrise ceremony at 5:30 a.m. Friday welcomes the day. Later, hula will be performed. Hawaiians will demonstrate ancient crafts. Kupuna in full regalia will offer opening prayers. Stimulating 90- minute discussions will take place on everything from the sensual meanings in hula to tourism and culture. In my view, this continues to be one of the premier cultural events on Maui.

One of only four resort cultural advisors in the state, Nae'ole has a heritage that uniquely qualifies him for the job. Some 210 years ago, a Nae'ole ancestor was a warrior king so trusted by Hawaiian royalty that he was charged with bringing up the future great King Kamehameha I, uniter of the Hawaiian Islands. Yet the usually mild mannered, now spiritual Clifford almost turned his back on his own culture.

Growing up near Waihe'e, north of Wailuku, on the taro fields farmed by his grandfather and father, Nae'ole remembers running through taro patches and picking huge sweet guava off the trees, playing in the mud and having fun while his hardworking parents did the tough work of putting food on the table.

After graduation from high school in Wailuku, Clifford was taken aside by his grandfather and told it was time for Kou Manawa, your turn as a hiapo (first born, first born, of first born) to continue the legacy of farming.

Clifford refused, aspiring to be a travel agent – an idea he later abandoned – and took off for the good life in California, where he married a lady from England. "Why did I marry her? Because," he joked, remembering his royal heritage, "England still has a king and queen."

When Nae'ole left Maui, he was told by his grandfather, "You've chosen to dine on the buffet of life." Coming back after 12 years, Clifford said, "the table was empty.

"The land was lost. It really hit hard, but what I have accomplished since would make my grandfather proud."

Nae'ole sought to find his culture, starting with hula lessons, then language, chants and finally embracing Hawaiian spirituality.

"My son was enrolled in Hawaiian immersion language school. One day he asked for help on his homework. His textbook was written in Hawaiian. I spoke zero. I knew aloha and mahalo and that was it," he explained. This is the man whose voice mail today starts and ends with Hawaiian. (Incidentally, he now considers himself a Kanaka Maoli—one, in his definition, who lives the old culture).

Clifford's renaissance—a work in progress, much like today's Hawaiian Renaissance of things cultural—is still underway because he says he still has much to learn.

Hired by the Ritz-Carlton as a telephone operator two weeks before the resort opened in 1992, Clifford took inspiration from the iwi, the bones of 2,000 Hawaiians whose discovery and preservation led legendary landowner Colin Cameron to move the location of his hotel.

Pushing the general manager to do even more by the culture, Clifford was quickly promoted to full-time cultural advisor—as he puts it, "the best job in the world."

"As cultural advisor, I have the opportunity to create bridges to reconnect the host culture to those we host (our visiting guests). I serve as the link between the Hawaiian community and the hotel on things cultural" he noted. This ranges from little things like correcting spelling of Hawaiian words on menus to supporting Aloha Festivals and this weekend's free Celebration of the Arts.

"Our purpose," he continued, "is to help visitors and those who live here understand our culture better through the lure of art, intellectual discussion, panels and films, music.

"There will be timely discussion of timely topics but no confrontation. Say to people what you believe, we tell panelists, but listen to others' points of view."

Nae'ole notes that Hawaiians "want understanding of who we are and what we can become, and understanding of the injustices that have been done and continue to this day.

"I am not a Hawaiian according to law. This hurts me deeply. You are a Native Hawaiian with a capital 'N' and capital 'H' only if you have 50 percent Hawaiian blood, and I do not."

Clifford added, "Those who are born here and choose to live here are part of the solution. If you are living in a gated community, the question is, are you keeping people out, or are you keeping yourself in? You worked hard and you deserve what you have but don't lock yourself out. My job is to tell a story and get someone to tell that story to someone else." The stories will be at the Ritz this weekend.

April 5, 2007

Postscript: A recent newspaper letter comments that the right to be called a Kanaka Maoli refers to those Native Hawaiians who have 100 percent Hawaiian blood. The writer points out that after a number of generations of intermarrying, a person with 100 percent Hawaiian blood could end up with six percent or less since each marriage to a Caucasian or member of any other ethnic group reduces the percent Hawaiian in offspring by 50 percent. This rule of life leads to the question, how much Hawaiian blood is needed to still be considered Hawaiian? Nao'ele's contention is that you are a Kanaka Maoli if you practice Hawaiian culture even if you are only part Hawaiian.

HOKULANI HOLT
Kumu Hula

The Role of Kuleana in growing up Hawaiian

"It 's time for all of us to stop and reflect upon all the great aspects that make these Hawaiian islands so special," Clifford Nae'ole, respected cultural advisor to the Ritz-Carlton, Kapalua," noted last week. "We need to slow down and get back to the basics." At this year's Celebration of the Arts, one of many speakers did just that.

Hokulani Holt, renowned *kumu hula* (hula teacher), grandmother, language specialist and cultural programs director of the Maui Arts & Cultural Center provided her own version of the basics by telling a charming, funny talk story well worth repeating.

Her talk, *"Kuleana* of Aloha," went beyond a common use of *kuleana* (taking care of the land) to a more fundamental meaning: taking care of and respecting people.

Those unfamiliar with *kuleana* think this is an amazing thing, she explained. "It means responsibility and accountability. What this tells us is we are held accountable for the things we do.

"If you were raised in a Hawaiian household, you know this from day one. You do this not because someone is watching, but especially when someone is not watching." Holt said her three children have *kuleana* in their lives.

"My oldest sister lives in San Francisco, never been married, has no children. We are her only "ohana (family), so to my number two, my son Lono, she is his *kuleana*. When she gets old, his kuleana is to take care of aunty.

"My younger daughter has me as her *kuleana*. This is the daughter; when I get old, she gotta take care of me. My other daughter, the eldest — and such is the life of the eldest — her *kuleana* is the whole family, the welfare of her brother and sister, her nieces and any children. Her *kuleana* is to make sure everybody is cool.

"You start when they are young — six, seven, eight, nine. Now they are in their twenties, nearly thirties, *kuleana* is a natural part of their life."

"*Kuleana* sometimes is seen by others as being burdensome, but its other definition is that it is a privilege. Think of all the times they took care of you. If you look at *kuleana* not only as a responsibility but a privilege, (you practice) it to the highest standard possible.

"In ancient Hawaii, this standard was very important. We lived right on the beach and we used to lay nets. The job of *keiki* was to clean the *limu* (seaweed) off the nets after fishing. You'd sit in the yard and you go over them inch by inch. Clean the net, repair the net, dry the net and bring it back to the net house and ready to go, because if the fish started running, you grab the net and got to go. If your holes were not patched when you took the net out you are not going to catch fish. And who suffers? Everybody."

By high school, Holt said teenagers are likely to complain that concepts of *kuleana* and adherence to rules are old fashioned. Holt told her own children, "This is not a choice; and there are many choices in life, but not these."

The same holds true, she said, for aloha — the love and compassion deep inside, at whose heart is the Golden Rule: "Do unto others as you would have others do unto you."

"It's what makes grandparents take care of their grandchildren, and grandchildren take care of their grandparents. You give aloha to others, you receive aloha. It's a cycle; aloha is given and returned, though not always directly. You do not just take, take, take."

Holt acknowledges that *keiki* learning to follow the rules sometimes require "a whack or two." She told the audience that "if you are in childhood education, sorry, but this works." In each generation, she noted, "Hawaiians who follow cultural tradition get a little more lenient. Yet a good many Hawaiians still bring up *keiki* in the old way. The evidence is there every day: friendly greetings and willingness to help, genuine affection shown with a kiss, sharing and giving, like Uncle George Kahumoku gifting anyone who visits him with vegetables from his farm.

Unfortunately, not everyone who has grown up or lives here follows these lessons. Young thugs beat up strangers, or there's yelling at visitors over trivial matters like choice beach parking stalls.

Kuleana, responsibility, respect, aloha. That's what makes Hawaii, Hawaii. We all win when we see it, lose when we don't.

May 14, 2009

KAHU DAVID KAPAKU
Minister

Pondering the Hawaiian God Ku and church

**Growing up in Honokowohau Valley, descended from a long line
of Kahuna (priests)** who paid tribute to Ke Akua (God), Kahu David
Kapaku knew at five years old he wanted to be a man of God. His grandfather named him David from the Biblical figure whose linage is traced to
Jesus.

During 12 years in college religious studies, Kahu David (Kahu means
minister) pondered the relationship between Christianity and Hawaiian
spirituality, concluding that the concepts of both are entirely compatible.

Hawaiians worshipped Ku Nui Akea (symbolizing stateliness and balance); Lono Nui Akea (the God of fertility), who Natives believed returned
in the form of Captain Cook in 1778; and Kane Nui Akea (symbolizing
life).

Christians have a Holy Trinity – the Father, Son and Holy Ghost – and
Hawaiians their own Trinity in the form of Ku, Lono and Kane. Hawaiians
thought their three deities represented the one, true God.

David noted that it is "kind of sad that Christianity has not embraced
many of the spiritual aspects of Hawaiians." When the missionaries arrived,
they found a fertile field among Kanaka Maoli who were already religious
and ready to believe in one God. Even some of the Hawaiian monarchs were
converted. Because spiritual Hawaiians didn't know Jesus, God the Father,
their concepts of spirituality early on were never embraced, David believes.

Hawaiian tradition includes stories of the flood (40 days and 40 nights,
instead of the recent eight days, seven nights here). In the Christian Bible,

Christ judges believers at the pearly gates. In Hawaiian tradition, Ku is also regarded as a judge, seeking to keep things in balance.

Ku often was considered a god of war. When land was snatched away from people unjustly, it was Ku who was looked upon to achieve balance and go to war to give it back.

According to Kahu David, some Hawaiians still believe in the old gods, including Madam Pele (the Hawaiian word for volcano) symbolizing land and its creation.

To Hawaiians, land is more important than people, with reverence for land still a driving force today. "People come and go. The land is forever," many Hawaiians believe. Hawaiian lands, especially Iao Valley and Honolua Bay, are considered sacred not because blood was shed there, but because both were the site of places of worship (heiau temples). There are an estimated 1,500 heiau sites on Maui and 1,500 sacred places, most of them still unidentified.

Every Friday, he and his Indiana-born wife, Kenda, sell baskets they make in their home in Honokohau Valley to visitors at The Westin Maui.

They weave them in part to keep in touch with Hawaiian tradition. David plays the ukulele, sells the baskets and frequently engages his customers in conversation about his most important mission: spreading the word of God.

December 6, 2007

KEKOA MOWAT
Security Man

Telling the tale of Keka'a

Five-hundred years ago, Keka'a village, with 10,000 souls, stretched from today's North Beach beyond the old "Airport Beach" all the way to Canoe Beach below the Hyatt Regency Maui Resort and Spa.

There was no Ka'anapali Beach. One of the world's greatest, most famous beaches was known to Hawaiians as Keka'a, a name that survives only on the curving road down the hill from Honoapiilani Highway to Ka'anapali.

The real Ka'anapali was further north, but resort developers liked the romantic name so much they renamed Keka'a as Ka'anapali, according to Kekoa Mowat and Krislyn Lavey, tour guides extraordinaire.

This little secret is just one of the tales told as part of the two-year-old Ka'anapali Historical Trail and Legends Guided Tour for locals and visitors sponsored by the Ka'anapali Beach Resort Association.

Boarding the Ka'anapali trolley, wearing walking shoes for strolls where sugar cane plantation camps once filled the landscape, locals and visitors alike joined guide Kekoa and his partner in a two-hour journey into history. Legends came to life as the rich history of those who walked these sands before us were explained with verve and enthusiasm.

Listen as tour guide Kekoa explains:

The pie-shaped village of Keka'a extended from outer reefs through fertile lands extending all the way to the mountains. Ho'okipa, the constant sharing of food and resources in which everyone gave generously of what they had, was the way of life. Fish brought from the sea were shared with those above who had bananas, sweet potatoes or taro.

Wood for canoes or spears harvested from higher elevations, or medicinal plants, were constantly exchanged for limu (seaweed) or shellfish gathered on shorelines where newcomers now stroll.

Thatched huts where Kupuna watched children while their fathers and mothers worked stretched to the horizon in a self-contained district where a proud and industrious people shared freely of what they had.

Children were often the product of temporary unions, with the motive of bringing forth children who would be of a higher class. "Kind of like the '60s," Kekoa noted.

Overlooking the Royal Ka'anapali Golf Course, Kekoa and Krislyn act out the legend of Moe Moe. Responding to requests by his mother, whose tapa for cloth making was not curing fast enough, the demigod Maui journeys to the peak of Haleakala to snare the sun and bring it across island to dry the tapa.

Maui asks his human friend, Moe Moe, for help, but Moe Moe prefers sleep. Maui turns him into a large flat, now sacred stone.

The huge stone sat in peace for centuries, if not eons, until the building of Ka'anapali Resort. The heavy, sacred rock is pulled by machine from a hole for a swimming pool. The next morning, it mysteriously is back in the hole. Two more times it is removed.

After each night, it turns up back in the hole. Modern man gets the message. The stone is carefully placed in a new location with a clear view of the sea and a special blessing ceremony held. More than 30 years later, the stone of Moe Moe sits in the same place, back to sleep.

According to Hawaiian values, it is important for people to have a sense of place, explained Moloka'i-born Kekoa, through the telling of legends and exploration of history. "We were never taught about our culture or the history of Lahaina in school. We're doing this now so students and locals can get more knowledge about places we pass by every day," he explained.

After growing up on the beach in Moloka'i, boarding at Lahainaluna High School, playing football – "We lost the championship game even though we were up 14-0 with a few minutes to play."

Kekoa graduated in 1988 and then stayed after marrying his Maui-born high school sweetheart. Six years ago he joined the Hyatt, moving up to the post of director of security and safety and having his boss volunteer him for the guide program.

Like 16 others from the Hyatt, Ka'anapali Beach Hotel and Westin resorts, Kekoa took 40 hours of classes in Hawaiian culture from Maui Community College's VITEC and even got drama lessons to help him act out the legends.

Key to the program's start were Shelley Kekuna of the Ka'anapali Beach Resort Association; Karee Carlucci, now executive director of the Lahaina-Town Action Committee; VITEC's Lois Greenwood; Alice Luther, director of the Maui Language Institute; Cultural Resource Specialists Luana Kawa'a and Kea Hokoana; and Lynn Britton, now in charge of MCC's West Maui Education Center.

March 1, 2007

Entertainers,
Entrepreneurs
and Colorful
Characters

PART 1

RUDY AQUINO
Entertainer

Star showman brightens Ka'anapali nights

Mr. Enthusiasm Rudy Aquino performs close to the audience to gain rapport Strong musical tradition in families brings talented performers to visitor venues throughout the island.

Just a few hundred yards beyond the beach at Ka'anapali, tucked below stately palms and winking stars, a five-minute stroll from the crowded restaurants of Whalers Village lays "a secret garden" – a Hawaiian garden. It's easy to find, but in some ways it's a garden often overlooked, even as it remains one of West Maui's most joyful places – the stage at the Ka'anapali Beach Hotel.

Strumming his uke, pounding on a vibraphone, joking with "the folks," master musician Rudy Aquino has been transforming the center courtyard into a magical oasis of aloha six or seven nights a week for a remarkable eight years. The masterful showman entertains from 6 to 9 p.m. for diners, drinkers or anyone who wants to sit and watch, free of charge. All comers are welcome.

Guests and regulars appear night after night, or return year after year, to partake of Rudy's musical talents and gift for gab that first gained prominence with the legendary Don Ho. One never tires of stopping by to hear his incomparable vibes and uke playing, and lively banter that varies little from night to night but never fails to captivate.

The most intriguing thing about Rudy is his enthusiasm, on display almost daily alongside his various partners, including Smiley Yoshida, Buddy Jantoc, Ernie Paiva, Ron Hetteen, and others.

Big Island born, Rudy took up piano at ten when his little sister quit $8 worth of piano lessons on the tenth session. Rudy stepped in at his family's insistence to take the last six lessons. He was hooked.

After his first paid performance at 15, he played honky tonk piano, the vibes, and percussion instruments at jazz clubs in Old Waikiki and later Hilton Hawaiian Village. "I was underage in those days, so I had to stand in the sand at the Garden Bar and jump over the wall to join in," he explained.

Rudy is quick to report that "when our group, the Ali'i's, started with Don Ho, we got equal billing. I will say that again. We had equal billing."

Draft age during Viet Nam and not interested in toting a gun, Rudy at 22 took his little group and auditioned – as amazing as it might seem – for the U.S. Air Force Band. The Air Force liked what they heard.

They said yes, Rudy enlisted, took eight weeks of basic training in Texas and was shipped to Washington, D.C. to play gigs along the East Coast. The highlights included playing for President Kennedy and Jackie at the White House and for the Mercury astronauts.

To make a long career short, Rudy performed on Johnny Carson's "Tonight Show," in Las Vegas and in California. Burned out after playing for Don Ho in the 1970s and '80s, Rudy settled in Maui in 1988, built two houses and worked for True Value Hardware in Kula. Missing music, he returned to the stage, ending up at the Ka'anapali Beach in 1998.

The Rudy show roars to life with a hula show — usually performed by his wife, Kanoelani; her daughter, Maile Lani; and Ula Nahooikaika.

Following a "short break," Rudy may impersonate Elvis, add papaya lyrics to a Neil Diamond song, play the Hawaiian Wedding song ("Honeymooners, come on up"), play classic Hawaiian songs, famously render "Phantom of the Opera" on vibes and even provide cha cha, waltzes, rumbas and more for dancing under the stars.

In light of the Iraq war, where his son once served, each performance ends with a rendition of "God Bless America." Visitors from around the world often return to the dance floor to sing and hold hands. Said one twenty-something honeymooner from upstate New York, "Rudy is phenomenal. He appeals to young and old."

For his spirit and his tales of Hawaiian culture, one is tempted to call Rudy "Mr. Aloha." Yet the real core of Rudy is that he is Mister Enthusiasm. Leaning on the Tiki Bar with coffee one recent morning, he said, "I don't know why I could do it so long for seven nights a week. Something happens on stage; it pushes me. I step on the stage and see people's smiling faces." The smiles are put there by Rudy.

The show ends with cries of "hana ho" (Rudy earlier in the show has taught his new-found fans that it means, do an encore.) At 65, Mr. Enthusiasm has no plans to stop playing. To Mr. Rudy Aquino, we wholeheartedly say, "Hey Rudy, hana hou!"

October 6, 2006

PART 2

RUDY AQUINO
KANOELANI AQUINO

Vibraphonist/Dancer say good night folks

"Hey folks, we are going to take a short, short break here and come back with our beautiful hula dancers with a nice Hawaiian hula show for you folks. Mahalo and aloha. What a crowd!"

For 15 years – in one stretch seven nights a week for 52 weeks – entertainer, vibraphonist, uke player, and joyful and enthusiastic dispenser of funny lines Rudy Aquino has been wowing visitors and locals alike at Tiki Terrace, Ka'anapali Beach Hotel (KBH).

Joining them in a farewell performance next week will be his favorite beautiful hula dancer, Kanoelani, Rudy's wife of four years. She's completing 15 years on the Tiki stage, including 12 straight years performing nightly.

To considerable sorrow from faithful followers – some returning year after year to stay at the place where Rudy plays and Kanoelani dances – they will be moving off to "semi retirement" to their beloved Cook Islands, a three-hour flight from Tahiti.

Happening on the pair being interviewed for this column, Robin Kart of the San Francisco Bay area told the couple: "We could stay at the Four Seasons or anywhere, but we have stayed here for 11 years because of your warmth. You've made us feel like family. And you are so genuine. You are not doing this because you get paid. The warmth we see comes from within, from your heart."

Though Kanoelani usually speaks with her hips and hula hands, here she talks story, with an occasional pidgin sound mixed in. Born and raised in Japan and China, a Navy brat whose father was a pilot, Kanoelani always knew she would wind up in Hawaii, site of many childhood visits.

Kanoelani earlier on was fascinated with Polynesian culture and wanted to learn as much as she could. At 21, she spent six months in Samoa picking coconuts on a plantation before moving to Maui in 1970.

Legendary Kuma Hula Emma Sharpe, once the sole performer of hula at the growing lineup of hotels in Ka'anapali, taught Kanoelani for five years. The songs and hulas performed by Emma remain alive to this day, becoming the model for the nightly shows of Kanoelani and her KBH colleagues who also dance.

Kanoelani lived right next to Sharpe in Kahana and had the task of sprinkling her large lawn – hard work in those days before automatic sprinklers. Kanoelani got respite from this daily chore only when it rained.

With rain clouds coming, Kanoelani would shout for joy. Thus, Emma gave the Caucasian girl who dances with the grace of a Hawaiian the name "Kanoelani," which means mists from heaven.

Kanoelani danced at Cooks on the Beach at The Westin and the old Kapalua Bay Hotel, where she met future husband Rudy Aquino, then playing cocktail lounge style piano at the hotel bar. Together, in 1992, they began their 15-year gig at KBH with Kanoelani in later years sometimes dancing alongside her daughter from her first marriage.

Just before Christmas, Rudy and his 'ohana were on hand to see another classic Rudy show that included his signature "Twelve Days of Christmas" with papayas and myna birds substituted for hens of laying and turtle doves. The song – sung hilariously with the help of 12 keiki, each with a part – was Classic Rudy at his entertainer best.

And that is what Rudy considers himself – an entertainer. In just a few sentences, he explains the philosophy that he tries to teach others.

He says there are two types of performers – musicians and entertainers. "If you are a musician, old school thinking says you belong in a chair with notes in front of you and a conductor. You cannot just take an instrument and play for yourself. You have an obligation," he explained.

"Some people save their whole lives to come here. What a blessing to have them here. So you have an obligation to entertain them, make them happy and comfortable. You go on stage and there are real people out there.

"You don't stand back; you step right out three feet in front to engage them. You joke with them, you recognize where they are from. You have fun. And you are an entertainer." It is a sad task writing a final tribute.

Perhaps the best end is to quote just a few words from classic Rudy: "Hana ho. Hana ho means to do it again, folks. We are going to do this song for you with a fast beat. This is called 'I am Hawaii.' Thank you so much for joining us here this evening. How about a nice hand to Kanoelani for dancing for all of you?

"Before we go, first, we have been having a lot of fun tonight, but we cannot help but recognize all our troops who have been working hard for us. We end every night with this song all about freedom. So, folks, sing along with us: GOD BLESS AMERICA, LAND THAT I LOVE"? "Goodnight Folks and ALOHA."

January 3, 2008

WILLIE K
Performer

Wondrous Willie K revealed

Slack key guitar is put aside for the ukulele at which Willie is equally adept.

The guy who is perhaps Maui's most talented, versatile and popular entertainer as well as once-time Hawaiian Grammy nominee often asks during his performances. "Are there any Willie K fans our there?" Usually, the crowd goes wild.

Google Willie K, short for Willie Kahaiali'i, and you'll find 150 entries—stories, web sites, links to amazon.com, CDs ripe for purchase and more. It would seem that with all the words written about Willie there would not be much more to tell, but there is—much more.

Willie K, now approaching 50 and new father of his fourth child, now eight months old, strums at lightening speed and plays on guitar or uke almost any kind of music (Hawaiian, falsetto, jazz, Rock and Roll, blues, R&B., Broadway, and now opera).

He has shared stages with Jimmy Buffet, B.B. King, Bonnie Rait, Mick Fleetwood, Crosby Stills and Nash and Prince and nominated for a Hawaiian music Grammy. He could be equally as famous nationally as the stars he has played with if he wanted to be.

Willie the last few years has come into his own not only as a musician but as a performer. At eight he played on stage for the first time and was immediately hooked. Asked if he strummed much in high school, he said, "Oh yeah, and in elementary school too."

Some thirty years ago, this son of Lahaina went to San Francisco to learn to play rock and roll. "All they wanted me to play there was Hawaiian music, " he joked in an all too short interview. Learn rock and roll, and much more, he did. With his musical apprenticeship complete, Willie returned to Maui in 1990.

He's been here ever since except for musical forays to perform on the mainland, China, Japan, Guam, Tahiti, Israel, Italy and Germany. He goes back to Germany on a six-city tour in May.

Maui's luck is that Willie rejected the allure of national stardom to play a number of years at Hapa's in Kihei, at the Maui Cultural Center, Mulligan's on the Green and numerous other venues here.

Rarely appearing in Ka'anapali the last few years—at 14 he played at Sheraton's old Discovery lounge and at the former Maui Surf—he now has a two-hour weekly Tuesday gig at the relocated Rusty Harpoon at the entrance to Ka'anapali Beach Resort.

Why does Willie live, play, write and produce music on Maui? His response is a rhetorical question: "Would you want to live anywhere else?"

Today, Willie has a new twist. Although his joy has been to play whatever he wants and play and play and play, he also now talks story during his two-hour show, regaling audiences with funny tales about the early days in Lahaina or experiences on stage. Example: "Once I was playing Georgia and someone asked if I was from the South. And my response was, "I hate playing in South Kihea (on Maui)."

Willie's personal hero is his father, Manu Kahaiali'i, a crooner but giant of a man at 6 foot four who supported many Hawaiian causes and did the Jackson Five with Michael Jackson eight better. Manu had all of his 13 keiki, with Willie the second oldest, perform on stage. The family work ethic—practice, practice—was a daily requirement.

The talented Manu exposed Willie to Don Ho and George Benson. Willie went on to spend eight months listening to and emulating the many styles of guitar great Joe Cano. In high school he also mimicked his idol Jimmie Hendrix even to the extent of learning to play guitar with his teeth.

"Are there any Willie K's out there? Eric Guilom, also a fast strummer who partnered with Willie for awhile as the "Barefoot Natives," is one. Playing with Willie is "like playing one on one with Michael Jordan," he has been quoted as saying.

At the Rusty Harpoon, the music soars, feet tap and the laughter during Willie's talk stories would do justice in quantity to a TV laugh track. There is only one conclusion: The wondrous Willie K, a musician's musician, through his talk story, has also become a comedian.

April 16, 2009

Postscript: The Rusty Harpoon, a Ka'anapali institution, for at least three decades, moved to a new location in 2009 and late in the year closed due to lack of business.

WILLIE K
Contributor to Community

"Let's get that canoe into the water!"

"Are there any Willie K fans out there?" From his weekly gig at Mulligan's on the Blue to the First Annual Gathering of the Voyagers on Dec. 5, the question posed by Willie Kahaiali'i is always the same. Last April and this December the crowd as usual answered with cheers.

At the gathering at Kamehameha Iki Park, Willie played for two hours, strumming the usual "Moloka'i Woman," an energized "Winter Wonderland" and singing a mesmerizing "Oh Holy Night."

The very busy, highly talented entertainment icon ("Beyond the Beach," April 16 issue) is much more than a music man, however. At the last Whale Fest, Willie told a packed audience: "I am out to save the world." Read on...

Willie grew up living in a kind of shack near a mango tree (one of the subjects of the many songs he has written). For years he played for what could be called a pittance. Today, with good paydays, he no longer has to worry about money and chooses to give many performances for free to benefit good causes.

He played on a cold, cold night at a festival for Women Helping Women. This fall, he sponsored his sixth annual Willie K Charity Golf Tournament, luring in celebrities he knows to play to help cancer victims.

Three years ago, Willie was named president of *Hui O Wa'a Kaulua* (Assembly of the Double-Hulled Canoe), a group formed way back in 1993 to build the *Mo'okiha O Pi'ilani*, a 62-foot voyaging canoe. Now, Willie is also a man with a mission.

He said he wants to bring better understanding of Hawaiian culture and its rich heritage to both Hawaiians and newcomers. He even wants to bring this knowledge to the rest of the planet through his international appearances. One of the means: the canoe.

Eons ago, Tahitian sailors guided by the stars journeyed all the way to Hawaii in double-hulled canoes. To show that two-way voyages celebrated in Hawaiian oral traditions could be done without instruments, The Polynesian Voyaging Society — made up of people from throughout Hawaii and elsewhere — built the *Hokule'a* and sailed it from Honolua Bay to Tahiti and back.

Moloka'i's Penny Rawlins — who, like many Hawaiians, was never given a Hawaiian name, because years ago this was not the fashion — crewed on *Hokule'a*. She also took the stage at the Lahaina concert to benefit the hui and regards the voyage as a life-changing event for her.

"When the Hawaiians sailed into the harbor at the end of their spiritual journey," she told this columnist, "we were greeted by 15,000 people (on the shoreline). The first words we heard were, 'Welcome home.' "

Descendants of Polynesians in Hawaii had returned from whence they came. Penny Rawlins Martin has been teaching Hawaiian culture since that journey.

"The canoe is like an island," she said she realized. "You have to learn to live together and make the most of your resources. You have limited water. The canoe is like magic. My mission is to teach the culture and the environment. I teach about trees, streams, forests and the land. Kids love learning about it. They are interested in all aspects of the culture."

Lahaina's canoe is a replica of the *Hokule'a*. To Willie, building and sailing it is a way to restore Hawaiian culture to its rightful place. Three years ago, with the canoe far from completion after more than a decade of delays, Willie stepped in to provide focus and used his considerable influence to get things done.

"This canoe is for all of Maui County — not just for Hawaiians but for everybody," Willie told the audience. "We all are trying really hard. We are just trying to make everyone in Maui aware. I do this (concert) for free. I donate my time just to make sure this happens. To me, this is one of the most important charities to be for.

"Don't be scared (to participate) We have people from Oakland to New York City cleaning up this place (Kamehameha Iki Park, where the canoe is being built). Very few come from (our community). Now you have been here, so you have no excuses because you know.

"As president of this *hui (partnership)*, I say thank you very much for all of your help." Then back to the music. As the last applause faded, one guest said, "It's been a long time since we came together like this as a community."

The spirit is there. Let's work to get that canoe into the water..

PART 1

GEORGE KAHUMOKU JR.
Taro Farmer

A Grammy award winner lights a fire

Doing many of the things that Hawaiians have traditionally done, including fish, farm and play music, three-time Grammy Award winner George Kahumoku Jr. has had a life full of choices. He could have been a successful artist or a prolific farmer, or a teacher who could use his skills in art to boost the confidence of troubled high school students, or an itinerant player of music, or a big name entertainer. As a matter of fact, he now is all of these, all the time.

Always reinventing himself between struggles to make ends meet, after a bout with cancer at age 27, the energetic and genial Kahumoku, 58, normally gets only three hours of sleep each 24 hours – a good thing, considering his many interests.

Growing up with a large 'ohana (family group) near Kona, amid 26 cousins, this mostly Hawaiian (amazingly one-eighth Mongolian) was constantly exposed to music.

"My great-grandmother used to make a drink called white lightening. That was our opportunity. They would pass out, and we would grab their instruments, go into the forest with a kerosene lantern and we would play music for hours," he explained.

Taking numerous detours after graduation from Kamehameha Schools in Oahu, Uncle George finally figured out the best way to make a living was to play music at the venues along Ka'anapali, including an early gig at my personal favorite, the gorgeous but short-lived Peacock restaurant atop Keka'a Drive.

In 1992, George began playing at The Westin Maui, with one memorable, funny result that had nothing to do with music. Living at the hotel, in an ultimate clash of cultures, Kahumoku and Hawaiian friends one afternoon decided they had enough of restaurant food. They would revert to their Hawaiian ways, grab nets and go fishing at Pu'u Keka'a, known to legions of visiting snorkelers as Black Rock.

Bringing along handfuls of peas, like those used by visitors to attract fish, Kahumoku and friends cast their nets and pulled in a mother lode of uhu, manini, kala. aholehole, u'u and others. Figuring they should avoid cleaning their catch at The Westin's spacious pool, they returned to their room, filled up the bathtub with fish for cleaning and flushed the entrails down a single toilet until it clogged up.

The fish would have to be dried. They strung up ropes, lined them with fish and turned on the air conditioning. Odors of drying fish wafted through the entire floor – the fishermen didn't realize the AC vents circulated air from one room to another.

Time to cook: gather dried kiawe wood stacked outside the Villa Restaurant. Find some rocks around the waterfall. Group the rocks into a small roasting pit on the fourth floor lanai, and lay a wire shelf from the mini-bar across the rocks. Fire it up – barbecue a huge kala fish on the open fire. Then walk down the beach before a Hawaiian supper.

The sirens of fire engines are not often heard along Ka'anapali Parkway, but they were that day. Yellow-coated firemen strung up a long ladder to the room to put out the tiny flames amid the rocks, blasting a big hole in the sliding glass door with the powerful stream. Another day in paradise.

The story is told in "A Hawaiian Life," the self-published book George sells at his slack key performances. Such mischief has been a way of life for a man whose infectious laugh is duplicated only by his wife, Nancy, the sister of his first music publisher.

In 1990, at the Mauna Kea Beach Hotel, management insisted George play with a partner. To keep it in the family, he picked his son, Keoki. Hands shaking, playing poorly, Keoki barely made it through the first set, supplementing his poor playing with an even worse voice. No worries.

"At the break," George wrote, "I grabbed Keoki's ukulele, used my wire cutters and clipped each of the strings on his instrument. From a distance, you couldn't see they were not connected."

The two "played" like that for months, musician and pantomime in perfect harmony. (Despite the rough start, Keoki today is a slack key master and Grammy winner). Then a flash of insight. Why not duplicate on Maui the successful concerts George appeared in on the Mainland? Stage your own weekly concert series and charge admission.

Paul Konwiser, a retired computer whiz with NASA and big fan, put together the first show. Clifford Nae'ole, the able cultural practitioner at the Ritz-Carlton, Kapalua, offered an auditorium. The Masters of Hawaiian Slack Key Guitar Concert Series was born.

Five years later, George and as many as 20 guest artists a year are still going strong, recently completing their 244th performance at a new venue, Napili Kai Beach Resort. Dancing Cat Records came calling a few years ago. Impresario George Winston regarded George's "melodies and his voice as a gentle Hawaiian breeze."

That breeze, plus the slack key music of a dozen others the last few years, has brought three Grammies and a recent nomination for a possible fourth. George plays on, when he is not planting taro or fashioning a ceramic. But that is another story.

November 26, 2008

PART 2

GEORGE KAHUMOKU JR.
Taro farmer and teacher

Hawaiian and man of aloha

Uncle George tends his goats on weekends.

Standing alongside his favorite goat near lush rows of taro and sweet potatoes, farmer, teacher, award-winning musician and composer George Kahumoku Jr. reflected on a versatile life.

"My music makes the most money, teaching makes the second most money, and the farm always loses all the money," he said.

But life to George isn't about money; it's about farming and giving back.

Precocious even at four, a keiki who loved to sketch horses on his parent's farm, George won his first scholarship to attend classes at the Honolulu Academy of Art in 1954. More scholarships followed to Kamehameha Schools and then the prestigious Rhode Island School of Design.

He skipped Rhode Island for a full scholarship at the California College of Arts and Crafts in Oakland because it was closer to home. The talented artist, trained as a sculptor, ended up after graduation teaching art to kids in the inner city.

He turned them off putting graffiti on walls and on to painting giant murals on downtown buildings with permission of an enlightened landowner. City officials were so impressed with this son of Hawaii that they made him art commissioner for California's Alameda County, including Berkeley.

Then opportunity knocked twice. Kamehameha Schools wanted him back in Honolulu to teach art. The job fell through, but he got a reprieve with an offer to start and become principal of a new Kamehameha Schools facility on Hawaii Island near the legendary City of Refuge. Struggling to make ends meet, he enthusiastically signed on. Ever restless, however, that, too, yielded to still another lifestyle.

Kahumoku started a farm on Hawaii to raise 1,200 pigs a year. This, he found, was a quick way to go broke, which he did. No matter. Lifestyle change three brought him to Mauna Kea Resort, where he began playing slack key guitar.

When the hotel closed for repairs, it was time for still another change: getting music gigs all the way from Ka'anapali to Kapalua where there was more opportunity. Maui's gain, Hawaii Island's loss.

George's slack key style dates back to paniolo days on Hawaii Island, when the cowboys played guitar to soothe cattle driven down the mountain to market. Loosened strings on a slack key can produce 80 different tones. The blend of two or more slack key guitars tuned differently produces an incomparable sound.

By the 1990s, George was playing 15-20 gigs on Maui a week and traveling to the Mainland, playing at performing arts centers as far away as Carnegie Hall in New York.

Five years ago, George substituted multiple gigs for just one on Maui: the Wednesday Masters of Hawaiian Slack Key Guitar Concert Series now held at Napili Kai Beach Resort.

Recordings of weekly appearances by George and a dozen or more artists, including Uncle Richard Ho'opi'i and up-and- coming Peter deAquino, have produced three Grammies in a new Hawaiian music awards category. And a new Grammy nomination was received just last week.

Meanwhile in 1992, with "time on his hands," George joined Lahainaluna High School to teach. He began running an alternative education program for kids on the verge of dropping out. George's approach is motivation through unconventional teaching.

"It wasn't that these kids weren't smart. They just never got direction. There were kids giving birth to kids, or two parents together with six jobs with latchkey kids," he said.

High schoolers had to be flunking five of seven courses, have missed two quarters in a row from school, and been absent 44 days to join the program.

George uses art, cooking and gardening as teaching tools to turn the students on. "How many seeds can you plant in a square foot of garden? How many gallons of water need to flow? It's all math," he explained. Hundreds of kids now lead productive lives thanks to George's interventions.

Four years ago, George also became a "weekend farmer," building a new home on a 4.5-acre plot near Kahakuloa on the North Shore. In Hawaiian tradition, sustainable agriculture is a community way of life. George and scores of volunteers, including residents, his students and even Mainland visitors invited up for the day, have turned four acres of scrub into a cornucopia of agricultural riches.

There are 80 varieties of taro, 3,000 pounds of sweet potatoes in the ground, and 30 varieties of citrus. A man favoring superlatives, George claims to have 100,000 plants. Much of the output is given away, although taro for poi is sold at modest prices to his Kanaka Maoli brothers and sisters at ten distribution points around the island.

Back home in Lahaina, munching a succulent papaya from his farm, popping a slack key album called "Drenched in Music" in the CD player, a writer struggles to fashion a last good sentence about this amazing man. Finally it emerges. In essence, George is a Hawaiian and a man of aloha in the best sense of both words.

December 11, 2008

SHANE VICTORINO
Major Leaaguer

Years of the flyin' Hawaiian

Shane Victorino, dubbed the Flyin Hawaiian by a sports writer for his speedy performances on the base paths, has come a long way from being a Wailuku T-ballplayer who not only made it to the major leagues but has set records the last two World Series.

Shane for the last few years already has been a local hero, his hits and outs dutifully reported daily during the season in a "Maui to the Majors" box in Maui News. Come World Series time, after hammering 14 home runs, batting .293, pounding out 30 doubles and stealing 36 bases during the regular 2008 season, he got to see his name in 48-point type.

Victorino made his first official appearance after that series at Lahaina Cannery Mall when kids of all ages lined up to have him sign 300 or more assorted balls, hats, t-shirts , photos and even placemats, his beaming mom Joyce standing nearby.

Thanksgiving week, the mayor honored Shane with a special proclamation noting "this is like the American dream come true up from a dot in the middle of an ocean to be on a championship team." The mayor proclaimed:

"Whereas, Shane Patrick Victorino, a graduate of Wailuku St. Anthony junior and senior high school has won a multiple of championship awards in his youth in football, and track including breaking the state record in the 100 meters.

"Whereas, after graduating from high school in 1999 he was signed by the Los Angles Dodgers, played for a short time with the San Diego

Padres, and the Dodgers and since 2005 has played for the Philadelphia Phiillies.

"Whereas, in 2008 Shane was the first Phillies player ever to hit a grand slam in post season history and the first person to have a home run, a double and two steals in a single game he ended the post season with 13 runs batted in, a franchise record.

"Whereas Shane was awarded his first Gold Glove earlier this month as one of the top defensive outfielders in the National League.

"Whereas, the Phillies took the World Series title and with this Shane became Maui's first ever World Series champion.

"Whereas Shane is a role model of sportsmanship hard work and commitment to the youth of our nation and proudly demonstrates the aloha of our islands wherever he goes, I Charmaine Tavares proclaim (today) Shane Victorino Day.

Voices of Maui finally caught up with him for a brief interview. Yes, he did dream of playing in the big leagues as a kid. He started baseball by playing T-ball. "Most leaguers started out that way too," he said. "Even A-Rod (MVP Álex Rodríguez) played T-ball."

Shane said his toughest critic during his Little League and Pony League days was his Dad, current County Council member Mike Victorino, who instilled in him competitive drive and commitment to working hard—essential character traits for reaching the big leagues.

In minor league towns like Great Falls, Montana, Yakima, Washington, and Scranton, Pennsylvania small-town-bred Shane got a chance to adjust to mainland living before the bigger challenge of playing in big cities.

Breaking in at age 18, the 28-year-old Victorino apparently has learned to be unflappable, claiming not to have been intimidated by playing in big league towns like Philadelphia or before 40,0000 cheering fans in Wrigley field. Nervous he has been sometimes, but not very often, he said.

Today he makes his home on the mainland at a point midway between Philadelphia and Maui so he can have good access to both. He's still a bachelor but—sorry girls—the handsome, tall athlete now has a fiancé and marriage plans.

Shane wants to be able to play in the majors another 15 years. His only career goal "is to get better and better each year." He al so hopes to inspire Maui kids to follow in his footsteps.

Good naturedly and patiently signing just one more autograph, he doesn't seem to have changed by fame. Shane summed it up best when he is and how he feels when he said: "I like to thank the mayor, my family and all those who supported me throughout the years through thick and thin. Things are very good in my life. I can't complain—that seems to be my favorite line right now but what more better to say that I am a world champion coming from a place like Maui. You all jumped on my back and you all supported me and I jumped on your back with all the support and love that I got.

"Sometimes I am speechless. To be able to come back home and represent not only my family and my Hawaii on the biggest level—I can say that we all, not myself, not my family, but all collectively as an island and state are known as world champions. So why don't you give yourself a round of applause for being able to support me all these years . You guys came out cheered me on and we are all world champions collectively. "

Well said, Flyin' Hawaiian.

October 12, 2008, Revised January, 2010

Postscript: The Phillies went on to became World Series Champs. In 2009, fans named him to the All Star baseball game in July, 2009 and the Phillies again made it to the World Series. Shane batted a career high 292, hit 13 triples, 39 doubles and 10 home run and won a second straight Gold Glove for his fielding. This month, he won at $22-million, three-year contract extension.

PART 1

HUMBLE BLACKIE GADARIAN
Bar Owner

A boat yard and a bar

Blackie(left) and wife Sara (right) shown on a picture postcard complete with tiny dots from the printing process.

The best word to describe orange-shirted Blackie Gadarian — 87-year-old machinist, former bar owner, jazz buff and irascible writer of pithy letters to local publications — is colorful.

Growing up in New York City, Arsene Gadarian won the moniker "Blackie" because of his thick black hair (now entirely gone).

After World War II, Blackie started Blackie's Boat Yard in Newport Beach, California, later opening a second one on Maui in 1979. To paint his new boat maintenance buildings in California, struggling Blackie got some strange, lead-based red paint for free.

A year later it turned an ugly color, and Blackie was told the only new color he could paint over it was orange.

The orange buildings became a trademark and orange shirts followed, worn the last 29 years on Maui. (His closet now has 40 of them, and none of another color). Wife Sara drives him around in an orange golf cart and truck with an orange stripe and logo. Sara usually wears light blue shirts.

Blackie is most famous around these parts for Blackie's Bar, an infamous hangout on land that once stood in the middle of his boat yard near the current Shell station across from Lahaina Cannery Mall.

To build his bar, the innovative Blackie bought the top of Windsock Lounge, well known as the place to go to have a drink before boarding a plane at the old West Maui Airport at "Airport Beach" in Ka'anapali. Blackie wanted the bar, which he put on a truck and hauled to Lahaina, because it was the stomping ground of renowned bartender "High School Harry" Given, revered for his powerful Bloody Marys. Blackie's Bar kept the Bloody Marys and also added Sara's famous, home-cooked meat loaf sandwich ($5.50).

The colorful Blackie sprang from colorful parents — two Armenian guerilla fighters who had to fight their way out of Turkey to come to New York. Born in 1921, Blackie grew up at 23rd Street and Third Avenue in Manhattan, as well as on the edge of Harlem.

During the height of the Depression, he took five-cent subway rides to a trade school, where he leaned to be a machinist. After a first job in which he said he earned 11 cents an hour, he joined the U.S. Navy at the start of World War II. As an airplane mechanic, he served on carrier flight decks in the Pacific and also spent time in Hawaii.

Blackie apparently was somewhat of a hellion. When he tried to reenlist after the war, the Navy said it was willing to take him back only if he would accept a demotion. Blackie said no. For the next 20 years, the talented machinist worked on aircraft maintenance for Western Airlines in Los Angeles and a company serving private airplanes. Next came the boatyards in Newport and Maui.

Blackie's Boatyard, highly visible along Honoapiilani Highway, was on a landlocked industrial lot far from the water. While the yard never did well, the adjoining machine shop prospered thanks to a hotel construction boom. A good customer was the new Hyatt Regency Maui, with West Maui's only machinist supplying brass railings, parrot cages and other ornamentals.

Then in 1981 came the bar, started for fun. Blackie's love of jazz — acquired in the days when he hung out at Harlem's famous Apollo Theater — encouraged him to turn the bar into a popular music venue. Jazz music buffs began flocking to the bar four nights a week to hear top artists, including the likes of George Benson and others who would sit in with local groups.

Blackie's was a no-nonsense bar. You couldn't stop with just a drink and a meal. If you wanted to stay, you had to buy another drink and another. Blackie said so, claiming he did not want tourists lingering at tables. Fail to comply, and you would be escorted out.

"Many people today claim they were thrown out of my bar. But I actually only threw out six," Blackie said. (One was his brother.) Blackie's Bar closed 16 years ago. But Maui had not heard the last of Blackie.

July 24, 2008

PART 2

BLACKIE GADARIAN
SARA GADARIAN
Retired Bar Owners

It's Blackie against the world

Soft-spoken Sara Richardson Gadarian, who has lived here for nearly two decades, has been married to "lovable, humble Blackie" for 48 years.

When they met, she said, "I saw a feisty man – tall, dark and handsome. He had a wonderful sense of humor. He made me laugh and he loved music and the beach. And he was a wonderful dancer who could do the Lindy Hop."

The marriage has survived, in part, because Sara – owner of an infectious laugh – has a sense of humor, too. Behind the rough, gruff, seemingly unapproachable facade of former Lahaina bar owner Arsene "Blackie" Gadarian is "a man who is extremely gentle with the people he loves," Sara said.

"But usually it is Blackie against the world." Many KPOA listeners were introduced to humble Blackie by radio commercials featuring the iconoclast himself. "Blackie's Bar is for grownups. Leave your kids and dogs at the hotel. This is your wonderful, lovable, humble Blackie," he would say.

Blackie's own drinking was supposed to be legendary, but he had a trick up his orange sleeve. Customers would buy him drinks, and he would pour the contents down a convenient drain when they weren't looking. He claims his other secret was having more than two drinks actually made him sick.

Visitors to the beer, burger and jazz joint just north of town were first accosted by a special sign. Blackie explained, "Most tourists used to be told that the streets of Lahaina were lined with free coupons. And everything was aloha. We had a sign that said,

ALOHA IS A TWO-WAY STREET

IF YOU COME HERE AND ARE NICE,
WE ARE NICE.
IF YOU COME HERE AND ARE...,
WE WILL BE
(phrases unprintable in a family book)

Above a long stairway lined with photos of old shipwrecks, there were more signs and more rules:

PROMOTE SAFE BOATING.
STAY ASHORE AND DRINK
AT BLACKIE'S BAR!

NO PIPE OR CIGAR SMOKING PERMITTED.

KEEP YOUR FEET AND LEGS
OFF THE CHAIRS

IF YOU ARE NOT DRINKING
YOU ARE LOITERING!

On jazz nights, Blackie would open the show with a monologue. Now, with the bar closed since 1991, he's taken to baiting tourists – he does not call them "visitors" – many evenings at Leilani's on the Beach at Whalers Village Shopping Center.

Blackie, with a cane, and Sara stroll in. Bar patrons scatter, and the two get stools. "What else am I going to do? I am not going to sit home and throw bread to the birds," said Blackie. Outrageous things come out of Blackie's mouth all the time – best left unchallenged. Yet, for anyone who loves to debate issues, the cantankerous Blackie is a joy. Once accepted, he's fun to talk to, because he is well-informed and a self-described "news junkie."

Obama? "If he can't stop smoking, how is he going to stop the war?" Development? "We have people who gripe about too much development. 'It is too crowded.' When I was born, there were 120 million people in the country. Now there are 300 million – what are we going to do?"

At 87, Blackie Gadarian shows no sign of stopping. In orange shirt, when and if he reaches the Pearly Gates, he must consider one thing: "No loitering."

July 31, 2008

JIM KILLETT
Gallery Owner

An artful journey

As the art capital of the Pacific, Lahaina boasts more galleries per capita than anywhere. Had it not been for a lot of rain in Germany back in the 1970s, things might have been different.

Jim Killett, former small college football player, football coach in Okinawa of all places, ex marine. He along with wife Nancy, once a gymnastics coach, wanted to travel the world. Killett, a self-admitted conservative sort who started saving for retirement right out of school decided to take a risk and pour all of the Killett's life savings into a business. "It took guts to quit my job," he said.

It rained a lot in Germany and Killett took to watching a lot of TV, especially the hit show Hawaii Five O. Killett fell in love with Hawaii and knowing he could move anywhere, chose Maui. Landing in Wailuku with no job, he stopped by a real estate agent who was advertising for a salesman but found by a twist of fate he was out to lunch.

Killett then drove to Lahaina, saw the harbor, and knew he did not want to live anywhere else. An ice cream parlor and an art gallery were for sale but the ice cream shop was taken off the market. So Jim ended up calling Nancy back in Arkansas to proclaim: "We just bought an art gallery."

Jim knew nothing about art. "Lahaina Galleries had one painting for sale by David Lee, sold art prints, and even puka shells. In the early days,

Jim used to ride his bicycle along Front Street with the gallery open but no customers; when a customer entered, he'd hop off the bike.

Thirty one years later, Lahaina Galleries is one of the most successful businesses of its kind in the state with galleries in Lahaina, Wailea, and Hawaii Island, San Francisco, Newport Beach and Bend, Oregon where his son Beau lives and works in the newest gallery Lahaina Galleries today represents 21 international artists, many who live, paint or sculpt in Maui.

Three were born in Italy, one in France, one in Argentina. How did the former football and gymnastics teachers do it? Apparently with a lot of luck, good ideas, honest operating methods (some art dealers have been known for their crass selling methods).

Starting with the talented David Lee in 1970, the Killetts signed on two other budding starts, Paris-born Guy Buffet, known for the whimsical Parade of Cows, scenes of old Hawaii and Paris bistros, and marine artist Robert Lynn Nelson.

Lahaina Galleries was one of the earliest promoters of marine art, nurturing Nelsons career until he moved on with Jim's blessing to establish his own gallery. Buffet is still with Killett after all these years.

Lahaina Galleries has spawned many imitators, propelling LahainaTown from a place with only two or three places selling art to more than 21 galleries today. Another key move, initiated by Jim and the LahainaTown Action Committee's Joan McKelvey was the start of Friday Night as Art Night in which galleries host some of their artists and offer visitors pupus and wine.

Lahaina Galleries artists make up a true 'ohana, even dropping in on art night even when they are not scheduled to appear. On a recent Wednesday Art Night in Wailea, artists known as the Twins could be found explaining how the gilt frames they make enhance the renaissance style paintings the two collaborate on. In front of the handsome bronze Hawaiian figure, sculptor Dale Zarrella explains his technique.

Serigraphs start at $500. The most expensive art: $500,000 fashioned by the late renowned sculptures Frederick Hart heads. whose work graces the site of the Viet Nam Memorial in Washington.

Today Nancy Killett, vice president who has been involved in the business from the beginning, has a second passion beyond the gallery: she teaches Sunday school and is the very busy head of the Lahaina Baptist Church's Youth Group.

These have been and continue to be sunny days for the Killetts on Maui, with those rainy days in Germany long past. There are no more puka shells in the gallery and Lahaina averages only 12 inches a rain a year.

June 28, 2007

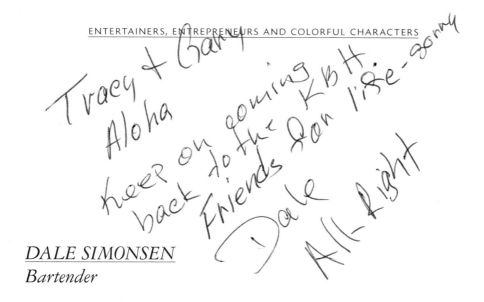

Tracy + Gary
Aloha
keep on coming KBH
back to the Don like
Friends - sorry
Dale
All-Right

DALE SIMONSEN
Bartender

The coolest bartender... 400,000 Mai Tais later

One fan calls him just about the coolest bartender on Maui. Thousands of visitors and locals know him only as Dale — the blue-shirted, congenial, low-key, easy-to-laugh purveyor of drinks at the Tiki Bar at the Kaanapali Beach Hotel.

Dale has a lifetime of observations on changing lifestyles and the habits of both visitors and locals that go back decades. He's been serving up drinks at the KBH (gulp!) for an amazing 40 years — diet cokes to Mai Tais, unique concoctions and everything in between.

Dale is so laid back he is an easy interview, talking in short phrases one morning as he mixed Bloody Marys and kibitzed with his regular customers, some of whom he has served for at least 25 years. His favorite phrase, though is: All...(pause) Right," often said after a drink is ordered or after a lot of other things. The conversation, recorded on tape complete with sound effects, went something like this:

Dale: Born in Oahu in 1946. Dad was in the military. Mom was a nurse at Queens (Medical Center). We came to Maui when I was three years old and lived in a little town called Pu'ukoli'i. I went to Kam III (King Kamehameha III School on Front Street) and graduated from Lahainaluna High School in '64.

I joined the U.S. Army and served at Fort Ord, California. I went to college, but I had to return because my mom (long divorced) hurt her back. Had to pay the bills (laughs). I got a job in construction. I worked on tiling at the Royal Lahaina.

Columnist: Did you set tile?

Dale: No, I was a mixer — a mudder (laughs). KBH hired me as a bellman in 1969. I worked nights. I was the low person on the totem pole (laughs). I started at Sugar Mill Lounge inside — on-the-job training. We had lounge music, and then a piano bar, and then went to local trios. The Tiki Bar opened in 1980 near the whale-shaped swimming pool. It replaced the Shipwreck Bar... Looking back, this job was a blessing. My life could have been working in electronics in California. I was very fortunate to be able to stay on Maui.

(Dale met the love of his life at work and figured it was about time he settled down. He married, had two daughters — now in college — and was widowed after 20 years).

Columnist: So what drink is your specialty? Dale: Anything is fine... almost anything (laughs).

Columnist: How have people's drinking habits changed over the years?

Dale: In the 1960s, it used to be Harvey Wallbangers, Tequila Sunrises. In the 1990s, it was beer and shots and then wine by people who thought they were connoisseurs. Word has gotten out about our Mai Tais. We were known for them. We also invented drinks. Tommy Rosenthal (Dale's long-time partner, mostly working the day shift) invented the Lava Flow (rum, pina colada, ice cream and strawberry puree). I invented the Ka'anapali Cooler: rum, orange and pineapple juice, blackberry and cherry brandy.

Columnist: What about the visitors? How have they changed?

Dale: Back in the '70s, people weren't rushed. Now they are always planning trips to Hana, but it's not long until they come back. People like the bar, because they have a birds' eye view of the pool and can watch their kids while they have lunch.

Columnist: What's the secret to making a good Mai Tai? How many Mai Tais do you make a day?

Dale: Probably about 40.

Columnist: That's 200 Mai Tais per work week, right? That's 10,000 Mai a year. And that is an amazing 400,000 Mai Tais during a career, and still counting. Miillions in bar tabs too.

Columnist: Have you served any famous people?

Dale: Julia Roberts. She played beach volleyball.

Columnist: Was Sarah Palin here recently?

Dale: That's right — after Christmas. The paparazzi showed up and she left.

Columnist: Did she drink

Dale: Not that I know of.

Columnist: Where do you live?

Dale: I have a house in Lahaina. Bought it in 1971 with my mom; three bedrooms.

Customer: I'll have a Bud Light.

Columnist: What makes a good bartender?

Dale: Show up all the time, and early (laughs). You have to be a people person.

Columnist: Do you think you qualify?

Dale: I'm working on it. You have to be a psychiatrist, but I don't give any opinions. It's like Switzerland back here. I am always neutral. If a guest asks what the weather will be, I say, "Well, forecasters often don't get it right. But my theory is it will be windy tomorrow." That way, the bartender doesn't get blame if the prediction is wrong.

Columnist: What do you do when someone is served too much?

Dale: I give them a warning. If they are using foul language and disturbing other guests, this is not acceptable. I don't like to do this when someone is having a good time. But there is a time and a place. The third time I say, "This is it," I confiscate their drink. And I give them a choice. I tell them, "I can pick up the phone, or you can leave. It's your choice." The good thing is, this does not happen very often."

Columnist: What about the people?

Dale: People love this place. Many come back year after year. You develop a friendship. Sometimes someone doesn't come back for 15 years, and you recognize him.

Columnist: Are you good at names?

Dale: Pretty much. But I remember faces. I've met thousands of people.

Columnist: So, are you thinking of retiring?

Dale: Not really... I'm going to continue

Columnist: Will you walk in with a cane

Dale: I won't go that far.

Columnist to a customer: So, why are you here drinking at 10 a.m.?

Response heard from across the bar: "Well, it's five o'clock somewhere."

Customer: I've been coming here since 2006. Dale is the best bartender on the Pacific Rim.

Columnist: How do you know that? Have you been to the Pacific Rim? What if there is a better bartender in Tahiti?

Customer: Well, I have been all over Hawaii. I guess he is the best bartender in Hawaii.

The morning at the bar goes on in similar fashion for a while longer, but you get the idea. In late afternoon, the columnist returns to take photos and meets still more fans of Dale."He is the best. He is attentive. You don't have to yell at him to get another drink."

And he knows what you like," said one.

Susie Johnson of Seattle (everyone at the Tiki Bar last Wednesday seemed to be from the Seattle area) said she has known Dale for 26 years. She said he's heartwarming, caring and fun.

Sharon Henderson chimes in, "Efficiency is good. He is efficient, too. A good word, too."

To top off the compliments, Johnson even noted that the previous night (mostly he works nights, but on Wednesdays, he works days), she and a friend even took took Dale out to dinner at Kimo's. And who does that?

Another guest had a final word. "You know, Rudy Aquino (before he retired) used to be Mr. Aloha around here. And now Dale is." Perhaps. But in this columnist's view, at the KBH he has a lot of competition from General Manager Mike White on down. And that's why you'll be reading a few more columns about the people at "The Most Hawaiian Hotel" throughout the year.

By way of disclosure, this columnist's view of the place is no different from dozens of people you can meet there every week. No money has changed hands, no favors granted, and there's no reason for saying so other than it's a fun place to meet people, listen to stories, enjoy music and sometimes even hand write a column or two at a courtyard table just before sunset.

And not to forget something, here a final "secret." Dale has a last name. It's Simonsen.

January 21, 2010

Postscript: An instant "celebrity," Dale began signing autographs on Lahaina News copies brought to the bar almost as soon as the column appeared.

PETER MERRIMAN
Restaurant Entepreneur/Chef

Pied Piper pampers patrons

Peter Merriman extolling the use of fresh fruits and vegetables grown by local farmers.

Working up an appetite? What better time than to visit popular and celebrated chef Peter Merriman, owner of one of the top grossing restaurants on Maui? Once called "the pied piper of Hawaii regional cuisine" by the Los Angles Times, Merriman teamed up with restaurant entrepreneur Rob Thibaut in 1984 to open the enormously successful Hula Grill, the Hawaii-themed restaurant just steps from Ka'anapali Beach.

The grill replaced the old Crab Catcher restaurant, still fondly recalled because tables were grouped around a decent-sized swimming pool. Our young kids splashed there as we dined.

Thibaut – "a genius and visionary," according to Merriman – provided a '30s Hawaiian-style beach house, including a barefoot bar with palm-thatched tables. Indoors, locals often sit in front of an open kitchen, dining while they watch a flurry of activity in front of them as the well-greased team of chefs cook on gas or wood-fire stoves.

Dollops of sauces are artfully dripped on big white plates soon to hold scrumptious creations.

Merriman provides an ever-changing array of dishes emphasizing seafood and blending Hawaiian, Japanese and Chinese cooking methods and local products that have come to be known as Hawaii regional cuisine.

Considered the co-founder of the genre, Peter found early success with locally inspired dishes and saw other chefs paying attention and embracing cuisine that the New York Times has said makes Merriman "a culinary renaissance man." He is, however, concerned about the future of his best suppliers. He feels the survival of farms is threatened by development that could take away acres of green farmland.

"I kinda don't want them to build bigger roads. The threat is we could lose the whole thing (meaning the beauty of Maui) if we are not careful. We have to decide where that limit is. We can't just keep going, going. I might be accused of drawbridge mentality, but so be it," Merriman commented.

The entrepreneur is also concerned about the availability of fish. In the old days, "fish was expensive because it was caught by a couple of guys on a boat." Now, even with mass production, fish remain pricey, because Merriman says we are running out.

"We have difficulty getting fish. There is always fish on the market, but a lot of fish is not caught in Hawaii. We are really worried about this," he said.

Growing up in Pittsburgh, Peter acquired his joy of cooking through his mother, a longtime food writer and city editor of the Pittsburgh Press. Starting as an apprentice at 16 and after attending college, Merriman went on to cook in Vermont, Germany and Washington, D.C. before being recruited to the Big Island in the early '80s.

My wife and this columnist met Merriman at a news conference for Maui County Fine and Fresh, a new program of the county Office of Economic Development to encourage people to buy locally produced farm products. Merriman had a lot to say, indicating he has been an early proponent of working with local farmers, because "when I was young and foolish, I was doing it partly for the environment.

Now I know that it is good business.", Turning to the lighter side, Merriman was asked about changes in the restaurant business.

"We started out with mostly seafood and steak. We were more Asian when we first opened, and we don't do much stir fry; we now offer more 'land' foods," he said.

Merriman sees changes in patrons, too: "The dining public becomes more sophisticated every year. There are more people who are adventurous and demanding than they used to be."

Also on the lighter side, Peter was asked for suggestions on how to cope with the many tempting food treats at holiday time.

He just laughed. "Ask my slim wife. If you want to eat, though, try plenty of veggies and salads – but they have to be flavorful. A lot of people send away for mail order beef. It's pretty fat, so you can slice it, eat two ounces and be satisfied.

When not working, Peter can be found spending time with his three kids, biking in Haiku and cooking. "I love to cook at home and develop recipes and new concepts that the talented chefs in my restaurants can refine, then add to the menus," Merriman remarked. So how good is the food at Hula Grill? I'm no restaurant critic, so you'll just have to try it.

December 14, 2006

Postscript: Peter Merriman has since opened a new restaurant in Kapalua called Peter Merriman's with renewed emphasis on utilizing locally grown fine and fresh products.

Islanders and Usurpers:
A Treacherous Tale

CAPTAIN COOK
HIRAM BINGHAM

Once upon a time there was an island

On the former site of the king's taro patch adjoining a picturesque harbor sits the Lahaina Public Library, repository of a two-shelf Hawaiiana section with books replete with tales of captains, kings, missionaries and creators of mischief. One book of note is "Hawaii: Return to Nationhood" published in—of all places—Denmark. The book draws a clear portrait of the tumultuous Hawaiian history of the last 250 years that still reverberates to this day.

In a move symbolic of the sensitivity of some issues, a library clerk even changed the book title, adding an identification sticker on the first page labeled "Return to Statehood" instead of the true title, "Return to Nationhood." A careful reading nevertheless inspired the following story:

Once upon a time—the year was 1778—a British sea captain named Cook landed on a majestic set of islands. Polynesians had discovered them thousands of years ago. The people he found were ruled by ali'i nui. The entire population believed in the philosophy known as pono, or righteousness—doing the right thing by caring for the land and its people and living in perfect harmony with the universe.

The people, as stewards of the land, knew that if they would ma'lama, or care for the land and its kalo (taro), the land would care for them and feed them. At a later time this concept of pono was turned into a motto "Ua Mau Ka Ea O Ka Aina I Ka Pono," the life of the land is perpetuated in righteousness. Even now this remains the official motto of the place called Hawaii.

Many moons after Cook died at the hands of natives on the shores of Kealakehua Bay on Hawaii Island, another sailing ship arrived carrying people known as Calvinists from a place called New England.

Cook, from England, viewed the natives as "a handsome people, hospitable, friendly and cheerful living in a beautiful land."

"These were a strong and hardworking people skilled in crafts and possessing much learning," another early observer noted.

The Calvinist leader from New England, however, described a different people—a people viewed as naked savages.

The Calvinist missionaries arrived shortly after a great king named Kamehameha died. Death had become—and would continue to be—a frequent visitor. From the beginning, the men who came in sailing ships after Captain Cook brought with them diseases. Early records are scarce, but typhoid fever arrived in 1804. Other visitors known as epidemics followed.

Influenza in 1826, whooping cough in 1832, mumps in 1839, leprosy in 1840, measles, more whooping cough and more influenza in 1848, smallpox in 1853, diphtheria in 1890, cholera in 1895, and even Bubonic Plague in 1899-1900. The epidemics attacked a susceptible native people, reducing their numbers. An estimated million native people dwindled to 200,000 by 1820, 40,000 by 1893, and fewer and fewer in the early twentieth century.

The missionaries brought with them wives and children and settled on coastal lands to preach the good news to the heathen natives. These Kanaka Maoli in many respects were as spiritual in their own way as their new teachers. And thus they became willing converts to the new religion. Missionaries told the natives that the tremendous loss of life resulting from natives worshiping the wrong God. The natives believed and the kings and queens led the way by converting to Christianity.

The missionaries also concluded that the Hawaiians needed a written language. They created an alphabet of 12 letters. The industrious Hawaiians, seekers of enlightenment, soon became the most literate people in the world as they read newly printed Bibles rendered in the new Hawaiian language.

Almost two decades after the missionaries first arrived a minister named Hiram Bingham declared that Hawaiians should abandon the concept of pono and make Christianity the cornerstone of their existence. He said old Hawaiian customs had to be abandoned. Christianity and capitalism, including private ownership of the land, would be what was pono.

A few years before, a William Ladd and Co. planted a promising new crop—sugar cane. What the new sugar cane growers needed more than anything was land. New arrivals viewed land not as Hawaiians did as a shared community resource but as a commodity to be bought and sold.

To grow the sugar, they needed to acquire a great deal of land, land that was used in common by the people and that no one owned. These newcomers, known as businessmen, pressured the king to declare what became know as the "Great Mahele." The kingdom's undivided land—4.1 million acres of it—would be divided up.

King Kamehameha III, considered one of the smartest of the monarchs, allotted the kingdom itself 1.5 million acres (36 percent). He allotted one million acres (24 percent) to himself. These became known variously as crown or ceded lands whose ownership sovereignty advocates are still fighting over today.

Just 84,165 acres, less than one percent of the total distributed landmass, were awarded to the common people and those who acquired plots got an average three acres each. Also, in appreciation for bringing Christianity and literacy to the islands, each missionary was awarded land too—526 acres each.

Some 1.6 million acres, or 39 percent, were converted into private ownership given to 251 ali'i (local chiefs), in effect allowing any of them to sell their holdings to anyone they chose. Many of the ali'i, who had acquired the habit of coveting foreign goods, were in debt to foreigners. Foreigners had the money. Ali'i had the land.

Through the Great Mahele and the associated Kuleana Act of 1850, foreigners were allowed to acquire land ownership for the first time. So-called 'ohana lands shared by the people could now for the first time be exchanged for money.

And so, it came to pass after a number of years, 95 percent of the cherished land came under the control of just 82 major private landowners, including many who formed what became giant companies, some still in operation today.

Britain and the United States also had their eye on the land, considering the islands a strategic place that could be used to protect and provide services for their interests in the Pacific. A Lord Paulett in 1843 declared the Hawaiian Islands a possession of Great Britain, starting a legacy that is still present in the form of a union jack on today's Hawaiian state flag.

Select numbers of Americans wanted more than land. They wanted control of the Hawaiian government. In 1893 they organized what in effect was a coup de etat to take the Hawaiian Kingdom away from a Queen named Lili'uokalani. In any amazingly speedy turn of events, a committee of safety falsely formed to protect lives and property during a period of supposed unrest called in the U.S Marines on January 16, 1893 to restore order.

On the 17th people who wanted to protect their business interests who were not Hawaiians declared establishment of a provisional government. Just 11 days later, after a long sea journey, representatives of the new "government" arrived in San Francisco on their way to Washington D.C. And six days later, they made it to the American capital.

Six days after that, a treaty of annexation bringing the islands under the control of the U.S. was introduced in the United States Senate. A representative of the United States to the new "government" in Honolulu named Stevens had opined, "The Hawaiian pear is now fully ripe and this is the golden hour for the United States to pluck it." In 1898 Hawaii was officially annexed and the progressive Hawaiian monarchy was no more.

Queen Lilioukilani, the last monarch deposed by the Americans, stands proudly near the site of the former palace and the modern state capital that replaced it.

In 1900, Hawaii became an official U.S. territory. And 50 years ago this month, it became a state—an action which most now feel worthy of celebration. After the land division, great plantation towns eventually grew up, filled with new immigrants—Chinese, Japanese, Koreans, Portuguese, Filipinos—to meet the demand for labor that could not be supplied by diminishing numbers of Hawaiians. Some 65,000 Asians alone arrived around 1890.

Twelve decades after the arrival of the missionaries came a rising power to the east who sent waves of war machines swooping in to strike a blow against the United States at a place called Pearl Harbor. Soldiers, sailors and marines came to help out their comrades. After four years of fighting throughout the Pacific, some stayed and some vowed to one day return, which some did.

On Maui, during all of this time, the land was transformed. Green waves of sugar cane covered the mountains. Pineapple fields blossomed with row upon row of succulent fruit grown, harvested and sent to big canneries that packed and prepared the yellow gold for shipment to what came to be known as the Mainland.

Finally, powerful winged craft called jet airplanes were invented, providing relatively easy access to this paradise in the middle of the Pacific. King Sugar gave way to King Tourism. Luxury hotels and condominiums and cramped quarters called time-shares arose.

Once-in-a-lifetime trips to paradise were turned into annual jaunts. The rich, famous and newly affluent came. They built million dollar homes where taro patches once flourished.

New lifestyles appeared, practiced by locals out of touch with Hawaiian roots and newcomers called malihina. Hawaiians, once told to abandon their customs, drop their language and forget their past began to recognize how much they had lost. And so began the "Hawaiian Renaissance" in which the native language and cultural practices were revived and new respect was given to the so-called host culture.

Once upon a time, a captain named Cook landed on majestic islands. It is still unclear whether the people lived happily ever after, or not.

August 16, 2009

Quality of Life

GORDON C. COCKETT
Former Police Officer/Retiree

Activist not going to take it anymore

Four years ago, Gordon C. Cockett decided he'd had enough. No activist for most of his 78 years, Cockett served in the Maui Police Department for two-and-a-half decades before retiring from the force in 1979 to ensure receipt of a pension.

Cockett then spent the next 17 years working for various restaurants and operating a fish market in Lahaina before retiring for a second time in 1995. Ten years later, everything changed.

"I really can't explain it," Cockett said of his new activism. "It was just something that got to me — all that traffic created by development. I got fed up with it — not only the traffic but everything else."

A modest, soft-spoken man, Cockett started speaking up at community meetings. Not long after, working on the theory that organizations advocating little or no growth need a united front, Cockett teamed up with Elle Cochran, first president of the highly successful Save Honolua Coalition, to form Maui Unite.

Maui-born Cockett, part Hawaiian, used to patrol Honoapiilani Highway when there was only one traffic signal on the island. Back then, star-studded nights were uninterrupted by the glowing lights, and green was the color of the great swaths of sugar cane swaying in the wind everywhere. In today's Maui, Cockett contends, the color green is mostly associated with money.

He believes developers are destroying Maui. These are not local people. They have come here and see the color green in the form of money. Greed is the driving force behind all this development — greed for money. The problem is you can't eliminate greed," Cockett said.

"I do not object to millionaires but I oppose million dollar homes," Cockett continued. "Millionaires generally don't come here to learn or live the culture. They come here to do their own thing. They want everybody else to abide by their own thinking. They want to change everything to suit themselves." Cockett knows the clock can't be turned back, but he believes that development should go no further.

"I care for this island. When I fly into and out of Honolulu, I shudder at the sight of houses on the ridges. There is a hierarchy in the Hawaiian culture that we *maka'ainana*, or commoners, belong down here. The ali'i (royalty) belong further up, and higher up are the deities, the gods," he explained.

Cockett came to his philosophy late. Concerned with making a living, he did not know much about Hawaiian culture. But one day he decided to learn. He struggled to learn the Hawaiian language. He met Kahu Lyons Na'one, an instructor at Maui Community College, and became a regular in his cultural classes, repeating the same or related courses 12 times to master the subjects and learn new things each time. This evolved into a belief about the importance of protecting land and preserving a Maui confronted with massive changes that have been rapidly altering its character.

Cockett is resentful of newcomers who want change, believing if they can't accept life as it is here, they should go back to where they came from. He cites the example of putting roadside memorial crosses near sites of fatal auto crashes. This is a Maui custom, but some newcomers regard them as unsightly and want them removed, he said.

The longtime Lahaina resident is upset about the power of unions to influence County Council development decisions. Although more building means more jobs, the reality is contractors often have to import construction workers from California to get the job done, Cockett believes. Sprawl, more infrastructure needs and limited jobs are among the drawbacks.

Cockett believes the Lahaina Bypass will spur further development: "I've never been in favor of the bypass road, but I have stayed out of it. It would benefit developers and development." He does not want a new four-lane road built.

"No way are you going to put that road up there," he has told the state. "But I wouldn't mind two more lanes along cane roads, providing two lanes in each direction." He claims County Councilwoman Jo Anne Johnson has said if the higher road is built, there would need to be roads for beach access every couple of miles. He believes this is precisely the kind of thinking that will lead to more development.

Cockett's Maui Unite organization has met with little success. Maui Tomorrow and the Ohana Coalition stand for many of the same principles he does, but so far Maui Unite has failed to unite them.

Cockett is quick to point out that he has not found answers to questions of development and jobs, but he soldiers on. "We have had enough development here. Let's stop. Let's slow down and take a look at where we are," he commented.

Cockett would like to be known as a person who cares rather than a person who is negative. "I fight development with the thought in the back of my mind that the harder I fight, the longer we will keep houses from being built on those ridges (above Ka'anapali and elsewhere)," he concluded.

No one knows whether development will stop, slow or continue, but Cockett is clear that he wants to protect Maui's environment and island way of life, declaring, "we are going to try. We are going to give it a shot."

June 11, 2009

SAVE HONOLUA COALITION

On behalf of my dear friend Honolua

Growth is inevitable. Or, growth needs to stop. This month, thanks to an amazingly fast-growing grassroots group called the Honolua Coalition, issues like these are being redefined.

One well-known former public official said, "The pendulum is now swinging. There is a groundswell of support (to limit growth), and the desire is becoming loud and clear. We have lost too much open space."

Maui Land and Pineapple Co. wants to build Maui's 18th golf course on Lipoa Point overlooking Honolua Bay, one of the most pristine and beloved bays on Maui along the coast past Kapalua. The conceptual plan for the area also includes 40 home sites mauka (inland) of Honoapiilani Highway.

Forty-nine community members from all age and economic groups spoke at a marathon four-hour session before the Maui County Council recently, saying "enough is enough."

Their arguments – some hard-hitting, others filled with tears – are compelling. Let's listen to these voices and try to find some balance between what they said and what might be possible.

"When you come around that corner, that bay, that beautiful water, it is like a clear diamond. We do not want to tarnish that diamond with another golf course," said Fred Vermey, ocean safety officer.

'We are turning back to ancient land ideas of those who were here first, to the Native Hawaiian understanding that we are not outside of nature but of it. Unborn generations have a claim on the land equal to our own.

Humans must learn from nature and replenish their spirits in frequent contact with the ocean. Each generation has a rendezvous with the land.

"We need to stop the tide of commercial development which creates an ever-increasing spiral of municipal costs. Once we decide that our surroundings need not always be subordinated to payrolls and profits based on short-term considerations, there is hope. The most valuable use for the land is to leave it as it stands, preserved for future generations to enjoy," said Brent Schlea.

"Change is inevitable. There was a time when we needed development for jobs and more opportunities. That time has passed. We are entering an era of accountability. Preserve open spaces for people and not profit," said Tamara Paltin, ocean safety officer.

"Where does the aloha come from? It comes from the land. Local people are saddened by what we see. Aloha is what brings visitors here; that's what makes this place special," said Kanoa Nishiki.

"To look out and see only trees and sky, to look out and to see beautify fish against a background of colorful coral, to be held in the arms of nature, to feel the love and maturity of spirit, the relaxation of the mind, the return of the child within. This is a priceless experience of nature that Honolua provides. People need beautiful places. Why not invest marketing money to enhance the product instead of paying ever-increasing advertising dollars to attract visitors," said Nikki Stange.

"Enough is enough; we need infrastructure We need a building moratorium. We need it now," said Doug Pitzer, general contractor and builder of homes in Kapalua.

So what is the right thing to do? It's clear that certain vast stretches of the island, particularly coastal lands, need to be maintained as natural or open space if Maui is to retain its all-inspiring beauty. And a "green line" needs to be drawn, allowing no further development above a certain level unless we want our mountainsides to look like Oahu's. Rural lands from the Pali, including gateways to Lahaina over one of the prettiest coastal roads in the world, should also be preserved.

Bowing to the inevitable, there are other places where further growth is perfectly acceptable — especially places where there is a need for affordable housing. In the best traditions of Hawaiian culture, it is time to bring things back into balance. Near the end of a long day, Jill Lassen testified: "I am here on behalf of my dear friend, Honolua Bay. Walking along the edge all the way to the Windmills (a surfing area), I hear her laughing. 'They do not have me yet.'

"And so," Lassen said, "close your eyes, all of you here, close your eyes, take a deep breath, uncross your hands and picture your most loved memory of Honolua Bay and feel it." She paused, offering two minutes of silence, uninterrupted by a council gavel. And to the council, she said, "Thank you."

May 3, 2007

VISITING CONVENTIONEERS

Fireworks, a logo and the spirits weep

Sensitivity to the host island culture took a hit last week. Pu'u Keka'a (Black Rock), our island's most western point, was revered by Hawaiians as a sacred place. Hawaiians believed that the soul leaped into eternity from this spot, known as ka leina a ka'hune. Those who lived here – with the exception of one brave ali'i, Kahekili, were afraid to dive from Pu'u Keka'a, considering it an offense to the Gods.

Jump ahead to late February 2007. Our public beach and shoreline is blocked by ropes and two courteous Maui police officers who tell everyone, "You will have to go around."

"Why?

"Too dangerous." Fireworks planned for later are implanted in the sand."

Jump to 8 p.m. or so. A huge T-Mobile logo, at least 20 feet tall, is projected with white light onto Pu'u Keka'a, the sacred landmark. Fireworks soon illuminate the sky only a few hundred feet from sacred ka leina a ka'hune. The assembled guests, brought to the Sheraton Maui for a gala dinner overlooking the sea and several days of fun and frolic as a reward for good job performance, gave the flashes of fireworks a big round of applause.

Maybe the swaying palms, wonderful setting, Hawaiian music and hula, and fine food weren't enough. It apparently was the logo on Pu'u Keka'a and fireworks that made the evening special. One can never, of course, get enough fireworks, even if everyone present has seen them scores of other times on the Fourth of July. "They were beautiful, weren't they," said one guest.

Last year, 40 members of the Maui affiliate of the Public Relations Society of America met for a luncheon program called "Doing Right by Aloha and Hawaiian Culture," featuring four prominent advocates of island values.

Tony Vericella, president of a Honolulu-based event-planning firm not involved in the T-Mobile event, spoke to the issue last fall, noting that meeting planners may not reside in Hawaii.

"Our job is to help them understand the culture so they do the right thing. We try to guide them. We absolutely will not do something if it is not pono, if it is not right."

He added, "We have something that is so special and unique that nobody has, and we need to share it in the right way, not give it away in order to chase the almighty dollar that sometimes people get caught up in."

Asked about the appropriateness of the logo on Pu'u Keka'a, Kupuna Ed Lindsey told this columnist that in western ways it is a cliff. "In Hawaiian ways, it is a graveyard. I don't know what their reasoning was, but they are jumping into darkness. It is taking from the host culture and not giving back for the purpose of marketing. In that light, it is an insult. The host culture is respected only when it is convenient."

Ironically, the Sheraton Maui makes an effort to celebrate Hawaiian culture with a nightly cliff-diving ceremony, includes a description of the history of the area and also supports a Ka'anapali historical tour.

Queried by this columnist, a spokesperson said the incident with the logo was clearly inappropriate.

"Never was there any intention, by the resort nor by the client, to be culturally insensitive," the resort said in a statement. "The Sheraton Maui Resort maintains a firm policy to uphold and respect the significance of Keka'a and the area surrounding the hotel."

JO ANNE JOHNSON
County Legislator

All "we do is talk, and no do"

Jo Anne Johnson. Kahu David Kapaku and newly elected County Council member Wayne Nishiki march in the King Kahmehameha Parade while expressing support for protecting the land..

Check out these excerpts from the letter below, which was written some time ago. And as Yogi Berra would put it, it is deja vu all over again.

Next, listen to some hard-hitting commentary from the woman who wrote it.

"The County Council and the Board of Water Supply seem to be headed down similar paths with regard to the increased use of an infrequently used planning tool – the moratorium.

"The use of moratoriums as a planning technique is often a wake-up call and a portender of serious problems within a community..."

"My personal belief is that we are on the brink of another surge in unchecked, infrastructurally inadequate and segmented development. The pressures that are being brought to bear on our community to develop our way out of our fiscal problems are tremendous.

When hotel moratoriums were previously enacted or when a moratorium was utilized preceding action on the Ag Bill, it was to allow time to assess the best course of action before proceeding. This is a prudent and responsible method of dealing with rapidly developing situations and it allows for both long- and short-term impacts to be studied.

"I doubt whether our infrastructure can withstand another sudden increase in development without experiencing severe adverse impacts. Kihei is testimony to our last real estate boom and solutions to their increasingly difficult problems are fast disappearing.

"With West Maui on the verge of beginning its community planning process and others nearing completion, we have an opportunity to scrutinize new subdivision approvals and major developments (hotels, large condominium projects, etc.) and their impacts on our infrastructure. Must we continue to grant approval after approval if we don't even know the cumulative impacts of segmented development, spot zoning or large-scale projects?

"Whether it is land, power, water, roadways or people, we must immediately initiate a 'carrying capacity study' and a 'needs analysis' for our entire county.

"Please look at both ongoing and pending development in Olowalu, Launiupoko and Ukumehame. The lands immediately mauka (inland) of the existing Honoapiilani Highway are largely zoned agricultural and have not been built upon as yet," the letter writer noted years ago.

"The Maui Long Range Transportation Plan leans toward eventual construction of a parallel roadway just mauka of the existing highway. However, as of this date, the Hawaii State Department of Transportation has made no attempt to acquire lands at existing agricultural rates.

"Please have the (County) Council consider passage of a temporary halt to new large-scale project approvals (possibly limited to certain areas) until a carrying capacity study and needs assessment can be completed. The pressure placed on the Council (as was done during deliberation on the agricultural bill) to act on this matter will force completion of this much-needed study in a timely manner, thereby allowing comprehensive planning decisions to take place, rather than limited reactive approvals."

Author? Jo Anne Johnson, private citizen. Written: June 19, 2000. Addressed to Wayne Nishiki, then a member of the County Council, now an activist supporting the Save Honolua Coalition.

Now skip to this Oct. 25, 2007, headline in Lahaina News: "Johnson proposes moratorium on agricultural lands."

This, it turns out, is the seventh time that three-term councilwoman Johnson has proposed a moratorium. And listen to what she said at an October community meeting, where she spared no words.

"Since I took office, I have had to introduce six moratorium bills. Now I am introducing the seventh," she said.

"Where is the political will? Where is the forward thinking? Maybe it is finally sinking in and a reality check is coming. Stop building altogether until we can figure out just what the devil we are doing," she said.

"I have begged for a hearing in the past, and I am going to beg again? I've been in tears because I have felt so totally frustrated? because I didn't think people were listening. Everybody is scared. All the developers show up, the unions show up (and say), 'Woe is me, jobs. We can't put bread on the table.'

"I have news for them. We can't even find workers for the jobs we have, so we are importing (workers). These new projects are all being done with crews coming over from Oahu or are being imported from the Mainland. We can't even find people to do our county projects. I am not buying that whiny little argument anymore.

"Get some courage and just move on it. The world is not going to fall apart. The economy will not go bust over night.

"First things first: in any business plan, you know where you are going and how you are going to get there. We never have a conversation about priorities. No wonder we are in such a mess.

"Let's have the (County Council) approach things in a logical, reasonable and accountable way so we have a plan. All we do is we talk a lot, but we do not do.

"You are not going to get to your goal if you do not know what your goal is. You need a plan to get there, and you establish a timeline."

Jo Anne says she feels like a broken record. And when she first started talking, they were records. Now they are broken CDs. Johnson is eligible for reelection only one more term, so she is convinced the time for a moratorium is now.

"If you repeat it often enough," she said, "if you practice what you believe in, you will get where you want to go."

To the community, she concluded, "Don't give up. Never, never give up."

November 15, 2007

DR. GEORGE LAVENSON
Retired Surgeon

"It's time for Maui citizens to unite"

When Dr. George Lavenson first came to Maui in 1963 as a vacation substitute for a local doctor, patients were seen from an office with an ocean view where the Hard Rock Cafe now stands. There was only one hotel in Ka'anapali, two good restaurants on Front Street and a bar across from the Banyan Tree. Lavenson, like so many others, fell in love with Lahaina and its laid-back lifestyle, charm and beauty.

Today, the charm and beauty, the semi-retired surgeon maintains, is not only being lost, it is being destroyed. A well-informed activist in the best sense of the word and a key player in the Maui Unite Group started by Gordon Cockett and led by dynamo Elle Cochran, Dr. Lavenson offers a blunt assessment of the current challenge.

The big issue is "unbridled over development." Lavenson says "there is not enough infrastructure for today, let alone the fact that we are now being over-urbanized." The doctor's thinking goes like this:

"Public officials approve all developments and always decide in favor of the power blocks: developers, landowners, unions and special interests. Developers are very good at mobilizing these groups. They even write out their testimonies for them. Members of the Planning Commission being advised by county attorneys believe they risk a personal lawsuit if developments are not approved.

"Meanwhile, the interests of the vast, silent majority, who love Maui and do not want to see it destroyed for selfish greed, do not appear to be able to halt it," Lavenson laments. "Developers and corporations want to increase revenues."

Unions are also culpable, saying they need the work, but developers import workers from Canada and Oahu. "It is a vicious circle. The more development, the more union work, and the more development is needed to keep them satisfied," according to Lavenson.

The Maui Unite member is especially concerned with a proposal to realign Honoapiilani Highway from Lahaina to Ma'alaea. "Landowners and developers," he says, "want to move the two-lane road mauka, high above the ocean. The reason is to allow development along the shoreline. The public would no longer be able to drive along the shore and stop and walk to any place on the beach, surf, fish, and paint or see either the makai (sea facing) or mauka views.

"The so-called parks that we are told will replace the old road are simply the ones already there with no assurance they would be kept up better than they are now. One of the most beautiful shorelines in the world would thus be destroyed, with development setting up a dangerous spiral in which West Maui would be completely ruined."

Lavenson suggests that campaign contributions to cooperating politicians give them a big advantage. "The only hope we have is to mobilize. One of the keys is the openness of Lahaina News and other media to present the peoples' side of the story," he concluded.

You can't fight city hall (in this case, the county) goes the old expression. Lavenson, an optimist, believes in this instance – given the willingness of people to fight for what they believe in – you can. It's time for the people to unite and get with it, he says.

March 27, 2008

CONCERNED CITIZENS

Keeping Maui paradise

"Affordable" housing on Maui these days, these are fighting words. County Council members like Mike Victorino, vote for more development because they will include some "affordable" homes. Some want to build "affordable" homes where the jobs are. Others, including people with deep roots here, want a building moratorium until infrastructure can catch up to the demands of an exploding population. And sometimes it seems as if class warfare is about to break out.

Here are some of the provocative things concerned citizens have to say: "The politicians are using 'affordable' housing as their excuse for voting for projects. We have over 22,000 units approved or pending here in West Maui and it is already much too crowded... There should have been, and should be, a moratorium, and no approvals, for sure, pending the Long-Term Plan.

'Affordable' housing sounds good, but it comes with the price of increased high-level development. Let's face it – not everyone or all the help can live in Beverly Hills. Council and commission members always vote for the developments, and all developments up to now seem to get approved. Public testimony is not listened to." – **Dr George Lavenson, retiree.**

"I agree with Mike Victorino (that) 'affordable' housing is sorely needed. It should be located where the jobs are, and that's why Ka'anapali 2020 is the most desirable location, just above the thousands of jobs at Ka'anapali Resort. The majority of workers live in Kihei and Central Maui and commute to Lahaina daily. That's estimated to be over 8,000 cars of workers that could be taken off the road if they could have an 'affordable' home in Ka'anapali 2020. Plus, West Maui and K2020 have water, and Kihei/

Wailea doesn't. Development is the only way we will get 'affordable' housing, because the county and state can't afford to do it." – **Joe Pluta, community leader**.

"We've got a lot of catching up to do, and we're not going to be able to if we allow development to continue the way it has. We must convince the administration and County Council of this, even if we have to march a thousand-fold on the County Building. Council members are divided into two groups. The voting majority votes pro-development all the time. The minority vote for what is best for Maui. Not all council members pay attention to what the 'concerned' public says. Only the minority does that. Others listen to their special-interest supporters, and that is why we have the problems we have today.

"We have more than our fair share of multimillion dollar homes. I am disappointed in our county government, top to bottom, which includes the administration, the Planning Department and Commission, and the major five council members.

They have all gone contrary to the island lifestyle of the local community by literally disregarding us, pushing us aside. The off-islanders who buy the multimillion-dollar homes are a different breed who don't want us makaainana (commoners) living amongst them. The developers add to this by trying to build 'affordable' homes in a light industrial area, instead of interspersing them in the common area.

"What's a matta – we not good enough for them? Why come here then? Mo betta they go Mojave Desert, where they can be by themselves and no need build 'affordable' homes. I'm not against millionaires living here, as I am not against their money. It's what they try to do to us when they get here. 'Where I come from...' doesn't fly in my space. One council person who came here from afar accepted the local lifestyle and learned as much as she could. She gets my vote every time." – **Gordon C. Cockett, longtime resident of Lahaina, former police officer**.

"I see our local residents frustrated and fed up with the direction Maui is headed. A new council will do our county good. Get rid of the majority of this council and vote in the new more Maui Nui (all of Maui) -conscious candidates. We need to get a well-rounded General Plan in place that will actually be enforced well into the future. Next, stop and take a look at where we are really in regards to land use, water, housing, infrastructure, marine and cultural resources, etc. Once everything is looked at and prioritized, then the decisions can be made as to what developments will be beneficial to

ALL – not just to the developers themselves and offshore investors." – **Elle Cochran, President, Maui Unite.**

"It seems that all we hear about is development, more development, but what about our infrastructure? We are so far behind in upgrading our sewage treatment plants, our roads, our schools, our water – how can one even consider building anything until we catch up? Maui already looks like Waikiki on the West Side, with all these new timeshare hotels built right up to Honokowai. The unions talk about more jobs. Yes, we will have more jobs, but the locals don't get hired. Illegals get hired; out-of-country builders get hired.

"The normal working person has no chance of buying anything, because the prices are so high. Victorino said people could buy a $300,000 home, but you have to have two jobs to do it. Is that what you call 'affordable?' To me, 'affordable' is a $150,000 home, a $100,000 condo. We better get back to the basics and think about our infrastructure and what we can do to improve it? I find it very ironic that of the nine members on the Planning Commission, four of them are realtors and one is a developer, and the vote always seems to come out 5 to 4 in favor of developing more hotels, high-end homes and condos. Election time is right around the corner, and I can only hope that we get rid of those that have done nothing for Maui." – **Ron Finer, concerned citizen.**

So the debate goes on – well worth it, considering the future of the island is at stake. One interesting question: If you could only build "affordable" housing, in the tradition of American ingenuity, would you build it or simply go elsewhere.

ROSELLE BAILEY
Homemaker
BRUNO" ARIYOSHI
Retired Principal

Ka'anapali 2020 trying hard to please

When Roselle Lindsey Bailey, part Hawaiian, descendent of an 18th century ship captain, joined the Ka'anapali 2020 community group in 1999, she was reluctant. Spirited even in high school, Roselle was among the small group in 1955 who began the tradition of lighting torches around the "L" above Lahainaluna High School to celebrate graduation. A one-time "stewardess" for Hawaiian Airlines, Bailey for a good 20 years served as "a plantation wife," raising three na keiki.

"As a Hawaiian and as an activist I joined (the group), but it was a difficult decision," she said. Her husband, along with many other employees, was let go with the closing of Pioneer Mill, "and it happened on my birthday. There was a lot of animosity," she added.

Roselle figured that she had nothing to lose and "could at least get out some of my anger."

Henry "Bruno" Ariyoshi, the descendant of Japanese grandparents and parents, grew up on the Pu'unene sugar plantation a few miles from the Maui International Airport. Fatherless at age four, Bruno went on to attend the University of Hawaii.

A 178-pound guard on the football team, he played in the legendary 6-0 defeat of powerful Nebraska before launching a career in coaching, counseling and administration. After a year in Moloka'i, he took the helm as principal of Lahainaluna, serving 25 years.

Both with deep roots in Lahaina, Bailey and Ariyoshi were well-suited to represent community thinking on what landowner Amfac should do with its 4,000 acres stretching from Honokowai to Lahaina Civic Center.

"There was a lot of ill feeling toward Amfac, so they started the 2020 process," Ariyoshi noted. JMB Realty of Chicago in 1988 bought Amfac, and its operations here are now known as Ka'anapali Land Management Corp. (KLM).

To reverse its fortunes, KLM took a bold step. Led by manager Scott Nunokawa, the company formed a 64-person group that met for "three solid days," as Ariyoshi tells it. "We looked at the past, the present and the future and what we envisioned 20 years down the line," he said. Eight committees reviewed such matters as transportation, land planning, affordable housing, education and health."

The citizens' group asked for land for a hospital, affordable housing integrated with market rate housing, an abundance of open space and a school.

KLM has accepted every idea but has been moving slowly and perhaps too quietly. The Ka'anapali 2020 project was not even included in the recent urban growth boundaries proposed by the Maui General Plan Advisory Committee. This unjust omission has been corrected.

The once-reluctant Bailey is now a strong Ka'anapali 2020 backer, expressing strong feelings about current development practices and rejecting the approach of some that she says treat land as "a commodity." In assessing KLM, she said it is an exception to what other developers are doing and way ahead of projects elsewhere. "We set the template (for what should be done)," she said.

Ariyoshi calls Ka'anapali 2020 "a wonderful opportunity for the people" and "a development process that would be hard to beat. There's been a lot of collaboration and open communication. "I feel very strongly that no other developer has done this. It's a good project, the vision is being kept and we are in good hands."

To be objective, Ka'anapali 2020 is not 100 percent pure. North Beach was sold to other developers, who have built towering resorts. If there is to be major development in these parts, better that it be planned with the community at the developer's elbow.

April 2, 2009

Paradox in Paradise
The times are a changing...

Fishermen still try their luck at twilight...

...but new uncontrolled development destroys pristine ocean views.

Young men still ride the waves daily late afternoons in front of resorts...

...as increasing traffic woes from burgeoning visitor counts threaten the old ways

JD and Harry Troupe (right) play Jimmy Buffet tunes at Leilanis on the Beach for locals and visitors on lazy Saturday afternoons...

...but young wahines waiting their turn to dance at the Ka'anapali Beach Hotel learn the hula at aone of more than 40 Maui halau (hula schools), beginning at the age of three.

Hula once banned still lives as Kupuna demonstrate their grace honed over many years

Despite all the growth and all the change, Maui remains Maui, a land of billowy clouds, deep blue skies, majestic ocean, frolicing whales and an aloha spirit you can't find anywhere else

The central question for quality of life: which voices will prevail? The voices of reason and Hawaiian values or the voices of unbridled change.

Who will step up? Those who destroy paradise by basing decisions on economics and the erroneous belief that more jobs are more important than the land?

Or those who understand that Maui thrives best when paradise stays paradise.

Which voices will prevail is still unclear. There are no easy answers.

*Movers
and
Shakers*

THEO MORRISON
Innovator

She jumps off cliffs

Theo Morrison couldn't be kept down on the farm. The self-proclaimed "cliff jumper" who left her Front Street pursuits to become a farmer four years ago is doing her special thing again, bringing fresh ideas and her can-do spirit to the Lahaina Restoration Foundation. Her newest commitment is promoting and preserving the history of Lahaina and enhancing this small town she loves.

Sailing from the West Coast, this one-time resident of tiny Ojai, California, arrived on Hawaii Island with two kids, an art degree and $1,000 in 1979. She rented a storefront for 200 bucks a month and built a successful business (employing six people) designing and selling artistic baskets. Then the market collapsed due to Philippine imports.

Moving to Lahaina, she soon was volunteering as president of Lahaina Arts Society. Not long after, in 1991, she pestered the fledgling LahainaTown Action Committee (LAC) to give her a job running the group that had created "Friday Night is Art Night" and an organized Halloween celebration.

Recalling that when she started, "I didn't know what I was doing." Theo found in herself a talent for learning along the way and getting things done. She had the all-too-rare knack for recognizing a good idea and relentlessly and passionately pursuing a goal by getting talented people to help.

During 14 years at LAC, Theo and a team of loyal volunteers managed or created 11 community events, including "A Taste of Lahaina and The Best of Island Music," "Maui Chefs Present" and the prestigious International Festival of Canoes. The spectacular success of these events – whose future is now in doubt – is well known.

By 2005 she passed the torch to others and left LAC for a new challenge: agriculture! Knowing nothing about farming, she nevertheless now successfully mothers more than 200 hens reared from mail order chicks. Twelve dozen eggs a day, plus asparagus, beets and carrots from her "Neighborhood Farm" are sold to Pacific'O Restaurant and several dozen neighbors.

For added income (while still farming), in 2006 she joined Lahaina Bypass Now dedicated to building an alternate route above Lahaina to relieve traffic congestion. Putting the organization on the map, she organized a transportation workshop that helped the Department of Transportation design future projects, installed bike racks throughout town, and pushed for and getting a new Lahaina bus route for local commuters.

When an opportunity to succeed Keoki Freeland at Lahaina Restoration Foundation opened up last fall, she couldn't resist. As the new executive director, she already has instituted candlelight night tours of the Baldwin Home and organized "Bath Day" to scrub Lahaina sidewalks. She's planning a Hawaiian music festival this March and a progressive dinner at historical sites to raise money for scholarships.

What makes a community treasure like Theo – who rarely ever says no – Theo? Vision, passion, tenacity and leadership. To organize the first "Taste of Lahaina," Theo and Kathleen Leonard, a friend, went to the newly opened Lahaina Center and boldly asked for $10,000 and the use of its parking lot. The center wanted a budget.

"We had none," Theo reported. Before Kathy could speak, she kicked her on her leg under the table. "No problem," Theo chimed in. The next day, they had their budget, and the event later went well.

Then Jerry Kunitomo of B.J.'s Chicago Pizzeria came along and pressed LAC to include music. Over the years, the event got bigger and bigger, achieving a peak attendance of more than 20,000. Whether there will be another "Taste," skipped last year, is unclear.

The canoe festival was born when Theo, Michael Moore of Old Lahaina Luau and Kunitomo wanted to stage a cultural event. "Canoes were important. Hawaii would not have been populated without them," Theo noted.

She wrote a grant for a street festival, and the canoe fest was on its way. The next year, Theo recounted, cultural practitioner Kimokeo Kapahulehua came along and announced at a meeting at Gerard's Restaurant: "Okay, this year we will cut down trees, get carvers, and make canoes."

"Everyone was stunned," Theo remembered. Kimo got beautiful logs from Kauai, and hotels were lined up to sponsor canoes. By the third year, the festival expanded to include a parade, launch ceremony, and music.

"Presented with an idea like this, people will NOT just jump off a cliff and do it," Theo said. "I am a cliff jumper. You don't need to know how you are going to get there. I am passionate about getting things done. It is so cool to come up with an idea, get a bunch of people together and make it happen. It wasn't just me. It was teams of people doing what it took. I think it's fun. I don't consider it work."

In essence, that's been her winning formula for success every time. Her strategies have been based on strong philosophies. Lahaina thrives by bringing people in to events that showcase its heritage, preserve its history and enhance the streetscape. She has certification from the National Trust for Historic Preservation in Washington, D.C., as a main street manager.

She has a philosophy about farming, too. "We need to demonstrate that sustainability is important and works. In the 1940s, we were self-sufficient here. This is the way it should be. Kids now think if it doesn't come in a package, you can't eat it."

Without Theo, Lahaina wouldn't be what it has become today. At college in San Francisco, later living in the country, and then in a small town, she figured down deep she was really a small town girl. Lucky for Lahaina, this is where she put down her roots.

It may take ten years, but I am going to prove there's a future in agricultural subdivisions," said Theo Morrison.

January 22, 2009

KEOKI FREELAND
Engineer

Fighting the good fight for Lahaina

Keoki Freeland – Lahaina-born, debonair in his broad-rimmed hat bedecked with a feather lei, three eighths Hawaiian, an engineer by training who has fallen in love with town history as executive director of the Lahaina Restoration Foundation – tells a story about the near death knell of LahainaTown.

In 1962, Lahaina was still a plantation town. Newly built Ka'anapali Beach Resort was pushing real estate values in town to unheard of levels. A few town "fathers" wanted to tear down all of Lahaina and build a new Waikiki.

Amfac, one of the biggest landowners and most enlightened benefactor, said no. Lahaina, the company believed, should be preserved as a historic town, as a magnet for tourists in need of more than a beach.

One large property owner in Lahaina was ready to sell out. But another said no. And up stepped Amfac, cosigning a note that allowed the second landowner to buy out the first, preserving Lahaina for future generations.

Soon after, people like Oregon businessman Jim Luckey, aided by an all-Amfac board of directors, formed the Lahaina Restoration Foundation

Two separate historical preservation districts were soon formed. The Baldwin missionary home on Front Street was restored so effectively that the powerful Baldwin family – still its owners – gifted the home to the foundation along with surrounding lands that are now home to Lahaina Public Library, an art gallery and parking lots. All contribute rental income that helps finance foundation efforts to this day.

But the fight for Lahaina is not over, as we shall soon see. And Keoki Freeland is in the thick of the effort to maintain, restore and interpret Lahaina.

Keoki's grandfather, a transplant who moved from Canada, built the Pioneer Inn, operated it until 1925, and fathered seven children with his full-blooded Hawaiian wife. Keoki's dad became a movie impresario, operating six movie theaters – one at Pioneer, and five on nearby plantations (a new feature every night, Filipino on Mondays, Japanese on Thursdays).

Keoki worked in the pineapple fields to get in shape for athletics at Lahainaluna High School. He said of the experience, "We tried to load those trucks fast so we could sit down and rest. But they would just send in more and more trucks! So we would load those buggers up."

Then it was off to college for separate degrees in mechanical and industrial Engineering – "I liked to be around machinery," he explained – and a 33-year career in the sugar industry. This included 21 years at Oahu Sugar and ten years at Lahaina's Pioneer Mill.

"When I started," he noted, "there were 27 plantations and 11,000 acres in sugar. Over time, Freeland designed machinery, became superintendent of field operations, and then first superintendent of both field operations and the mill, the number two position in Lahaina.

Along the way he married a native from Honokowai Valley north of Ka'anapali who was a descendent of Hawaiian royalty. It wasn't long before she took to putting paint to their drab plantation house walls. Thus began Betty Hay Freeland's long career as well-known impressionist artist.

With sugar on the way out, Keoki retired from the mill in 1995 only to see it close four years later. Before he left, he was instrumental in developing for Ka'anapali what he said was the world's first scientifically developed coffee, an effort only now paying off.

Recruited by LRF, Keoki asked why they wanted an engineer. "I thought these guys were nuts. I had no idea of town history, but I found it very interesting."

Under the 25-year stewardship of Jim Luckey, executive director emeritus and honorary director, and now Keoki, the foundation has flourished. It now manages nine historic sites, and has five museums, including the Old Lahaina Courthouse and Hale Pa'i, site of the printing museum.

The foundation wants to preserve the landmark Pioneer Mill smokestack and build a mini-museum around it. It needs an agreement from the current landowner. LRF needs the County Council to keep a promise to reimburse it for $300,000 it spent to correct major structural problems at the courthouse, its museum and gallery.

The foundation needs county funding for a historic preservation officer who would police merchants and make them follow preservation rules. The foundation need county funding for historic preservation officers who would police merchants and make them follow preservation rules.

And it needs color control. One merchant has painted his building pink – a preservation no-no. Keoki wants the county to cut red tape and put teeth into the laws to end troublesome violations.

Keoki, in the Hawaiian way, is currently working quietly on all these new problems, but so far with limited success. He won't say it, but this columnist will.

It is time for enlightened leadership – the kind we saw from the old Amfac years ago – to respond to Lahaina's needs and overcome obstacles that do not seem so insurmountable. Keep up the good fight, Keoki!

April 19, 2007

ELLE COCHRAN
Community Organizer

A skateboarder and surfer makes a difference

Daughter of Okinawan parents Elle Cochran has become leading advocate for preserving the land island wide.

In the instance of Elle Cochran, community activist, a profile seems to want to write itself. Such is the case with the founder of Save Honolua Coalition, who only needed prompting with a few questions. The answers tumbled out in short concise sentences one after another.

Cochran, schooled at Kamehameha III and Seabury Hall and married to surf shop entrepreneur Wayno Cochran since 1996, takes up her story in her own words:

"My first job was at 13 at Charthouse being a prep cook. One of my favorite jobs (at 16) was with Joan McKelvey at her South Sea Trading Post right on the ocean where Kimos is now...I have been pretty much a hard worker all my life.

My mom ran a restaurant and bar called Moki named after my Dad. Originally it was at 764 Front (Street) and we lived upstairs. It was such a fun, great town and everybody knew each other.

"We dove for coins near the old Carthagenian in the harbor. We would go, "mister, mister, throw a few coins into the water we will dive for them." That is how we made the money to go for our manapua (bread) at Hop Wo Store and shave ice with ice cream and cheeseburgers at the nearby Yamamoto's.

"These were the good old days in Lahaina and I can still remember them in my mind's eye. When I walk down there today there is no resemblance. It's kind of sad. Then there was liberty restaurant with its fried soup (thick blend of noodles).

We ate that every day. It was homemade and tasty. "My dad was a heavy equipment operator who built a lot of the hotels like the Sheraton. He passed away when I was three. My dad was Hawaiian, English and Spanish and my mom is pure Okinawan, born in Oahu of Okinawan parents."

Pausing to relate a story about how her brother died from either getting the bends after an unheard of dive of 300 feet or from an encounter with a shark (no one knows which), Cochran explains that the episode made her fearful of the ocean. Finally overcoming the fear, she took up surfing—a fateful decision that led to her marriage to Wayno Cochran.

Years before as a 10 year old she used to skateboard near his shop. He complained that he felt like he was running a day care center for kids. Later, nearly 30, she met him again as a surfer and asked him to shape a longboard for her. Dinner and a movie followed and in 1996 —despite a 15-year age difference—the two zipped off to Fiji for their wedding.

About 10 years later, Maui Land & Pineapple Co. asked Elle and other surfers for input into a surf park they wanted to build near pristine Honolua

Bay. "We loved that. Maybe a little cultural center down by the bay too. Sounded good," she said.

"But of course they failed to mention the 40 luxury homes they wanted to build in a gated community and the private golf course. I was pretty much the first person who wanted to do something to protect the bay from that massive development.

"What made me take a closer look was my husband got served when a sheriff came to our house with court papers. He has lived there for 40 years. They want to take us to court over land, take the land down by the ocean. It was then I realized there was something more to their plans.

(According to Wayno, the company owns a one percent interest in land he bought a few years ago. This gave it the right to force a sale, with the land to be sold at auction to the highest bidder. Cochran suspected the winning bidder would be Maui Land & Pineapple. A lawsuit over the dispute goes to trial in November).

To fight the proposed golf course on Lipoa Point, Elle and Wayno spearheaded formation of Save Honolua Coalition. "We went out and educated the community. At our initial public meeting, 45 people showed up at Farmers Market. Then we went to the Civic Center and that began to fill up. Web designer Shawn Reid popped up a website. The fire got lit and it spread (involving) people who have intimate knowledge and attachment to Honolua Bay. Visitors knew about it and people from all over the world.

"Then came six to eight hours of testimony before the County Council. We got all the kids out of school. It made a big difference hearing the keiki testify about what was going to be left for them. Kids in elementary school were worrying about their future. I was concerned when I was a kid about playing on the beach, not saving the beach. (Today's children) have seen so much loss (of free space) already.

"(The coalition caught fire) because of the subject matter. This was such a special place to a lot of people, worldwide. (Wayno describes it as one of the best surfing areas in the world). This was also about community. "

You've always got to let the community participate in figuring out the solutions and educate as to what development was about. Then they choose, for or against. From the mayor to the planning director, environmental people all came to our meetings.

The education was on both sides and many jumped on the bandwagon." Maui Land & Pineapple Co. eventually announced it would drop plans to build on Lipoa Point. The broader issue of what it can build, where, is unresolved.

Growing in knowledge and stature during the Save Honolua effort, Cochran has since moved on to continue to push for restrictions on development through a new group, Maui Unite, formed with Gordon Cockett.

All of this taught Elle perhaps her most important lesson. "One person can make a difference," she says. That is why I am planning to run to succeed Jo Anne Johnson next year on the County Council."

If elected, Elle wants to be collaborative. She currently is meeting with as many council members as she can to build relationships and help them get to know her.

With the incumbent prevented from running because of term limits, there should be stiff competition. Let the debate on who can best serve West Maui begin.

Postscript: After months of negotiations Maui Land & Pineapple Company has backed off of plans to develop Lipoa Point. New leadership at the Coalition is focused on compromise. The company—in exchange for not proceeding—wants concessions allowing it to build elsewhere. Current economic conditions have put any plans on hold.

JOAN MCKELVEY
Community Treasure

Remarkable Joan

Joan McKelvey engages in traditional sign waving with fellow supporters of her son Angus McKelvey. Angus won and is now up for re-election.

The remarkable, intrepid Joan McKelvey, still a premier mover and shaker in Lahaina as an octogenarian, rarely ever talks about the many things she has done during a long and colorful lifetime - really two lives in one, pre-Maui and post-Maui.

Australian-born Joan Howes McKelvey left school at 18 becoming a newspaper reporter for the Melbourne Argus, reporting, she said, about virtually everything.

Then it was off to Europe for more journalism with the London Daily Mail. Returning from a year in Morocco, she joined Wilson Harrell, a worldwide marketing company. She was soon promoted to vice president for the European Theatre and then the Pacific, becoming acquainted for the first time with Hawaii.

Somewhere along the line, she met the love of her life, A. W. (Mac) McKelvey, a dashing former Spitfire pilot who left for England to fight alongside the RAF in the air Battle of Britain before the U.S. entered World War II. Mac went on to fly for the U.S. Air Force, finally ending up on Maui.

He worked for Amfac as vice president of property, played a key role in developing Ka'anapali and later left the: company for other business ventures, including building the Lahaina, Ka'anapali and Pacific Railroad.

Mac discovered that vestiges of the old Amfac rail line that once hauled sugar cane to Pioneer Mill were still in place. From a conversation with former rail workers at Pioneer Inn sprang the ambitious project of building what became known as the Sugar Cane Train. McKelvey worked diligently to acquire numerous rights of way, hired gandy dancers who spoke 17 languages to build track, found and refurbished two steam locomotives on the Mainland and built passenger carriages named for Hawaiian kings.

Families with kids were soon riding the historic train listening to a conductor pluck a ukulele and sing songs of Hawaii as the train chugged along through seas of green cane fields beginning in the late 1960s.

The journey produced cherished memories, including some for my own family. The train still runs, serving 500,000 riders annually at its peak, though it has been sold to new owners many times.

As a businesswoman, Joan was busy opening and running the South Seas Trading Post in a series of shops on Front Street, later in Kapalua (now closed), in Ka'anapali at the Hyatt Regency and now again back on Front Street. Since opening it, Joan has journeyed to the Far East scores of times, gathering one-of-a-kind artifacts from Indonesia, Thailand, the Philippines, China, Japan, even the Himalayas. She just completed a new trip several weeks ago.

As a community leader, Joan has been active in Lahaina since the mid-1960s. Meet Joan casually, and you might never know of her many involvements. When Mayor Hannibal Tavares threatened to keep traffic away from Front Street in order to build a bridge, Joan, along with Connie Sutherland and Lynne Ho, formed the LahainaTown Action Committee (LAC), becoming its first president and later serving another term in the 1990.

The citizens' group open to Front Street merchants and any other locals who wanted to join thought the traffic diversion would be the death knell for local shops. The new committee won its case and the traffic diversion was avoided.

LAC, led for many of the most recent years by get-things-done Executive Director Theo Morrison, has built a remarkable record of success, often with Joan's ideas paving the way. First came "Friday Night is Art Night," the brainchild of Joan and Lahaina Galleries owner Jim Killett, which has now become a Lahaina institution.

Working with David Allaire, Joan and LAC soon took over the planning for Halloween, transforming it from an informal celebration into the well-organized event, with streets closed, costume contests, music and the maintenance of order by cooperating police.

Then Joan advanced another idea: a food festival. "A Taste of Lahaina" began as a modest Tuesday luncheon event. The weekend extravaganza now attracts thousands from all over the island to feast on the best offerings of a dozen or more restaurants, hear Willie K and other top musicians, and watch public officials barbecue.

Of all the things she has done, Joan is proudest of two. In 1994, Lahaina News - now thriving with essential reporting on West Maui concerns not covered fully elsewhere - was in danger of closing.

Joan organized a hui (partnership), enticing a dozen or more West Maui investors to put in $10,000 or more each, to buyout the owners, save the paper, and begin its revitalization.

She doesn't say so, but all those family political discussions around the dining room table she and Mac engaged in sparked an interest in government on the part of her son, Angus, to run and win election against an incumbent for the West Maui seat in the state legislature last fall. Already, he is scoring victories for Lahaina and West Maui, too. Her other son, Ian, is a certified pilot who runs a parasail company half of each year in New Zealand.

Joan turned 81 years young the first week of June. She clearly is planning on sticking around a lot longer. Her mom, still living, is 101.

Postscript: Taste of Lahaina ended its long run in 2007, a victim of both the economy and the fact it may have grown too large to be sustained in a small community. Eighteen years after helping found it, McKelvey is back as president. Today, she is trying to rescue Lahaina's famous Halloween celebration which has been somewhat curtailed by actions of a county cultural commission.

ANGUS MCKELVEY
State Legislator

Honolulu's Mr. Maui

Angus McKelvey, accompanied by State Senator Roz Baker, participate in a fall 2009 sign-waving demonstration protesting teacher furloughs.

To make ends meet, like many of his constituents, West Maui State Rep. Angus McKelvey has three jobs. He works 16-hour days when the legislature is in session and spends numerous hours talking story with colleagues and the people he represents. To serve the needs of his constituents, McKelvey has a salary of $38,000 a year—far less than members of the Maui County Council.

In job two, he is a freelance graphic artist for local publications and publisher of a pocketsize Lahaina historical guide, earning income by bringing in advertising revenues.

His third "gig" is with South Seas Trading Post, the retail shop owned by his mother, Joan. There he deals with customs issues, uncrates merchandise and does odds and ends.

Right out of college, McKelvey got his first job as a legislative aide in Honolulu – training he now puts to work pushing his own legislation. Swept into office with other first-time representatives – now collectively known as the "Gang of Nine" – the newcomers formed an alliance to help each other.

Soon, Honolulu began to pay attention to this brash 40-year-old. Colleagues dubbed him "Mr. Maui," because he seemed to be in their face at every opportunity to explain the state economic engine that is West Maui and its vast needs.

McKelvey has been instrumental in bringing legislators up to speed on the need for the island's second hospital to serve the 65,000 residents, commuters and visitors on the west side. A frequent visitor to the office of Department of Transportation Director Brennon Morioka, McKelvey has pushed hard to find innovative solutions to traffic problems.

He is proud of his initiative to establish Traffic Emergency Zones. This McKelvey bill passed into law but not implemented by the governor would have created traffic emergency zones that suspend various rules. The legislation cuts red tape, requires only federal permits, and allows cane haul roads to be used for emergencies. The bill was written for West Maui but would apply statewide.

The Maui Traffic Control Center bill provides for a $400,000 center to be run by the county to synchronize traffic signals to meet changing traffic conditions, and operate electronic signs (controlled by computer) to warn of traffic jams and road closures. Gov. Linda Lingle is withholding the funding for this bill.

McKelvey has also weighed in on alternative energy source. He says wind power is unreliable as an energy source because the wind often blows strongest at non-peak electric use hours. Wave energy is "firm" – consistent. Wave energy works like an ocean blowhole. Waves pounding into a closed chamber drive turbine blades. A McKelvey bill would establish such a system based on a successful concept working in Australia.

And he noted that the Maui delegation, supported heavily by influential Senate Ways and Means Committee Chair Roz Baker, has secured $80-million in funding for Kahului Harbor, the Lahainaluna High School cafeteria, a new Kihei high school, roof repairs at King Kamehameha III School and many other projects.

McKelvey said he chose public service because he thought, "things were going backwards in West Maui. We finally had good economic times that could provide for needed projects. As a state rep., I could really help this town out."

McKelvey has chosen to be very aggressive in pushing for Maui's needs in Honolulu, supported by a mentor, the wily Joe Souki, who McKelvey called "a real friend of West Maui." He notes that "my mom taught me that you always put your community above self, and this stewardship is what you will be remembered for," he said. McKelvey wants to serve more time in the House to finish the initiatives he has begun. Whatever path he takes, his future looks bright.

Postscript: Angus McKelvey is the son of Joan McKelvey, another Maui mover and shaker. Governor Linda Lingle has yet to provide funding for traffic initiatives.

JO ANNE JOHNSON
County Legislator

Going to bat for West Maui

Tending her e-mail, she sometimes falls asleep in her chair at midnight after a 19-hour day. "I will wake up in the middle of the night and say to myself, 'Why bother going to bed? I'll just get up.' " So it goes for popular, dedicated Maui County Councilwoman Jo Anne Johnson.

Her boss, she said, is the people who she serves full time — at the council, attending community meetings or pausing at the grocers to listen to a constituent's views before going home to make dinner. Though declaring "my work life is my personal life," no small part of it is caring for her husband, Jim, wheel-chair bound, mind sharp, fighting the progression of Parkinson's Disease. She still makes his lunch before heading off many mornings to Wailuku.

At the council, Johnson is also in a fight — a fight to serve West Maui and make sure it does not become another Oahu. In her three terms, she has persuaded the state to protect Honoapiilani Highway from wave erosion, got the county to build the start of Kiawe Street extension for the proposed Lahaina Bypass, and secured $1 million for Lower Honoapiilani Road paving and improvements.

She successfully fought to keep a shopping center from being built on a Lahaina historic site where King Kamehameha III once lived, and even helped kill an ill-conceived plan (for Maui) to build an attraction featuring performing dolphins.

Jo Anne believes building affordable housing for workers should be one of Maui's highest priorities and pushes such projects at every opportunity.

On the contentious issue of growth and development, she favors a moratorium on all development with the exception of affordable housing.

She believes "growth isn't necessarily negative and does not have to be feared, but it has to be smart growth — not growth whose only purpose is to create subdivisions and McMansions" crowded with homes, but remain green and beautiful, she believes.

Density, when needed, should be purposeful and integrated into the new County General Plan. It should set down fundamental principles and limits that need to be followed.

"We must look forward seven generations, which is a Hawaiian concept. If we do not do projects and land use planning that is pono (right and good), I believe we will ultimately fail in our efforts.

"To do things in the proper way, we need to act with respect for the host culture in all endeavors," she proclaimed.

Making sure the powerful, policy-making County Council acts in what she perceives in the proper way sometimes means that the Johnson voice frequently is a lonely voice. Some council members historically have not met a development they haven't liked, and they have voted accordingly.

While allies do rally around her, the challenge of putting together council majorities that support the Johnson vision often eludes her. She is the first to admit that to change the will of the majority on important matters is her biggest failure and frustration.

Though she gets along well with other council members, her biggest fans appear to be voters who have returned her to office five times in impressive numbers.

This session, Johnson wants for push for collection of new and previously authorized impact fees that developers can be required to pay to support infrastructure improvements. She is also pressing for quick action on the part of the council, as well as the Planning Department, to approve a zoning change that would pave the way for the building of the proposed West Maui Hospital.

So where does the fight for good things for West Maui, and Maui in general, stand? Jo Anne believes that "the community has reached the end of its rope. People want action, not just rhetoric."

The good news is that the County Council has three new members. As a veteran on the council, Jo Anne said it will take "political will." She is hoping that the new members will be willing to set priorities, be innovative in their thinking, accountable to their constituents and ask their communities to support their agendas.

She also sees the state being more supportive of West Maui's needs because of what is being called the West Maui "mafia" – powerful new committee chairs from Maui, including newly elected state representatives willing to be more proactive in the state legislature.

As she goes to bat for West Maui this year, Jo Anne is hoping to up her average. "I would like people not to give up hope. I will never give up trying," she concluded.

February 7, 2007

Postscript Jo Anne is still trying as she nears the end of a final term. With just a few exceptions, Council members elected in 2008 have kept to their old ways.

JERRY KUNITOMO
Restaurant Owner

Pizza King serves up best in Hawaiian music

When Hawaii Island-born Jerry Kunitomo first arrived on Front Street, little did he know that he would become a music stage manager and producer extraordinaire for "A Taste of Lahaina and the Best of Island Music," which was held for the 16th time last weekend. Jerry's mission was pizza.

The son of a Kona coffee farmer with deep Hawaiian roots and a third generation Hawaiian-Japanese mother, Jerry for 15 years made a living in Orange County, California. He studied architecture, opened a successful architectural firm and also had a background in fine dining restaurants in Huntington and Newport Beach.

But he loved the restaurant business, working first as a busboy and eventually winding up as a troubleshooter inspector for Tony Roma's restaurants.

Then he caught the eye of the founder of B.J.'s Chicago Pizzeria, a California restaurant chain that has since grown into a $1-billion enterprise.

Would Jerry journey to Maui to open a new restaurant? Jerry said yes even though he had never been to Maui. Bringing along his seven month-pregnant wife, Jerry was lured in part by his desire to bring his kids up Hawaiian and to teach them how to spear fish, as he did as a boy.

Jim and Nancy Killett of Lahaina Galleries expressed doubt that Jerry could succeed in a second floor location, saying, "Boy, you are a nice guy but it's too bad you signed a lease upstairs," as Jerry tells it.

Whalers Realty owner Bob Cartwright, picking up restaurant prizes for his annual golf tournament, once asked Jerry if the new business would last the year, citing his family rule that he would not dine with wife Tess in a new restaurant until it was a year old.

No worries. The deep-dish pizza patterned after pizzas made famous in Chicago by Gino's, Pizzeria Uno and Lou Manotti's caught on. The business thrived. And, years later, 1,500 pizzas a week come out of Jerry's ovens.

Just a year after baking the first deep dish, Jerry opened a food booth at the fourth "Taste of Lahaina," ferrying less-than-warm pizza from his restaurant all the way to the festival.

He soon told Theo Morrison, the brains behind the formation of "Taste" with LahainaTown Action Committee, that he could boost attendance by 20 percent by bringing in back-to-back acts of island music.

Today, food and music lure 10,000 to 12,000 to the event, and Jerry is still coordinating and masterfully staging the music.

"I felt local music would bring the locals, and the synergy of getting tourists and locals together would create an event that people would come back to year after year. Another key was to seek the support of KPOA's "Morning Goddess" Alaka'i, Home Boy and Uncle Poki to link up with the music groups and perform emcee duties," Kunitomo explained. KPOA radio has been an active supporter ever since.

Jerry's strategy was to get top musicians, treat them well and provide a great sound system in a gorgeous setting. His favorite moment? Placing the stage so the audience could see the famous "L" over Lahainaluna High School and watching the audience rise to sing.

Backing "Taste" with considerable dollars and his indomitable energy, it is the best-attended event in West Maui other than Halloween.

Jerry noted that the Lahaina community is unique with its willingness to volunteer, with musicians often willing to appear at less than their normal rates as their way of contributing to a good cause.

Jerry's community involvement did not stop with "Taste of Lahaina," either. Along with Theo, he conceived and created the International Festival of Canoes to bring Hawaiians back to Front Street and celebrate the islands' Polynesian heritage. The event has been called, by the master carvers who participate in it, the most significant annual cultural event in the Pacific.

Jerry's belief in community service knows no bounds. He once was on 32 different Lahaina committees, but more recently has scaled back.

One can debate all day what drives "Taste's" continuing success: food, or music? There is no doubt that the pizza king and his musician partners are are the ones who have made the "Best of Hawaiian Music" truly the best

September 20, 2007

Postscript: Times change. Taste of Lahaina and the canoe festival now are fond memories, casualties of the economic downturn and lack of complete community support. Jerry more recently changed the name of his restaurant to Lahaina Pizza Co. and is still serving thick Chicago style pizza.

PART 1

MIKE VICTORINO
Legislator

From baseball coach to County Council

You can see him on Akaku Maui Community Television almost every day trading wits with colleagues on the nine-member County Council. Unlike many of his colleagues, whose trips to our side are confined to official meetings, he is a frequent visitor, whether it's the Sacred Hearts School Bazaar or other events.

One of the many jobs he's held – sometimes two at once – was in security at the Ka'anapali Ali'i next door to the rapidly expanding Marriott Ocean Resort. And he is a friend of West Maui.

He is likable, outgoing Mike Victorino, a self-described blue-collar guy not unlike many of his compatriots on the council. If education is any measure of qualifications for office, Victorino has more than most. He's a few courses short of a degree from Maui Community College, having studied marketing, business management and personnel, and plans to complete his coursework one day.

Born in Hilo on Hawaii Island of sixth-generation Portuguese parents in Hawaii, Victorino moved to Maui in 1973 as assistant operations manager to help open up the first Zales Jewelry store at Queen Ka'ahumanu Center, eventually hoping to live and work in Oahu where the best jobs were.

He is still here after many stops – 12 years at McDonald's, running different units in Lahaina and the other side; then van driver up Haleakala Crater for Mountain Riders bicycle tours; and serving as a security man at hotels.

"My parents always taught us to work hard, take care of home, and never forget your community. You've got to be active, and I was," he said.

This has meant service with Jaycees; Knights of Columbus; Little League, Colt and Pony League Baseball; coaching at St. Anthony's; and volunteering 16 years on committees for the Maui County Fair, including nine years as director.

Running for council seemed to be a natural next step. Victorino said he brings to the job two essentials: love of the land — growing up on a farm with pigs, cattle and chickens, "where we learned the value of living off the land" — and knowledge of the tourist industry from his Mountain Riders and hotel security work.

"I felt I could make profound change for the people. We have a chance to make a difference right now," he declared.

Victorino said he was surprised at the learning curve involved, noting that he thinks four-year council terms would be better, since new members take awhile to get their feet wet. His big struggle has been balancing the need for affordable housing while avoiding development that contributes to what he calls "sprawl" (his views will appear in the next column).

Victorino said one of his concerns is that not enough has been spent on infrastructure, although he acknowledges the outrageous cost.

The first-time councilman, elected in 2006, was an early advocate of banning plastic grocery bags, a new law that goes into effect in 2011. Why not sooner?

"The people need to be educated on the benefits, and mom-pop stores need to work off their supplies," Victorino said.

On TVRs (transient vacation rentals), he said that Mayor Charmaine Tavares enforced the law — good, bad or indifferent — as it existed.

Asked why the council did not step up quickly to change the regulations after the mayor cracked down on rentals, he admitted, "it has been a slow process, but we are trying to do the right thing. We are working very diligently to get this done."

He wonders why there was plenty of water for irrigating thousands of acres of sugar cane, yet the county is facing a shortfall. "We have not done a good job managing water. We have the wherewithal to make these changes. I think it is really important," he commented.

Victorino disagrees with two proposed council reforms. He wants to continue one-year instead of two-year budgets, and believes the current election system — under which every county citizen can vote for all nine council candidates — should be continued.

Plugging away at the issues, this former baseball coach had no opponent for reelection to his Wailuku-Waihee-Waikapu seat.

He rarely makes headlines but sees the Victorino name in print nearly every day – on The Maui News sports pages.

Speedy Major Leaguer Shane Victorino, "The Flyin' Hawaiian," a kid whose favorite sport was once soccer, is batting .290 (14 home runs, 34 stolen bases) for the Philadelphia Phillies.

Dad catches him on TV or the Internet as much as he can, and sometimes travels to the Mainland for games. He'll fly to the World Series to watch him play if the Phillies get there. If the Phillies don't make it, he's rooting for the Chicago Cubs.

October 2, 2008

PART 2

MIKE VICTORINO
Councilman

Does he deserve a valentine or no

Mike Victorino will be reelected to the County Council Nov. 4. This is automatic, since Victorino is unopposed. Thus, we can delve into his views — that may not be all that different from other council members — without favoring one candidate over another.

One of the core issues now is the future of development, brought to a head by a vote on the proposed Wailea 670 project near Makena that has implications for all of Maui.

In a 5-4 vote, Victorino, Gladys Baisa, Mike Molina, Danny Mateo and Joe Pontanilla voted for the project, and West Maui's Jo Anne Johnson, Bill Medeiros and two who are not seeking reelection, Riki Hokama and Michelle Anderson, voted no.

How each member voted is significant, because under Maui's peculiar voting system, West Mauians can vote in all nine council races — even those for Hana or more populous Kahului.

Victorino came down on the side of approval, trying to balance his strong feelings on the need for affordable housing with his love of the land and, as he describes it, "protecting fauna."

He insists that more houses must be built, so young people can stay and not flee the island. Victorino also believes a $300,000 house is affordable for those who hold two jobs.

There were many people who testified for Wailea 670 and many against it, according to Victorino. He said he took his cue on how to vote both by listening to testimony and also through personal interaction with constituents. Many locals, he pointed out, are not all that comfortable speaking up in public.

To counteract this, he said, "I really listen when I go to parties, weddings, and baby showers. People say, 'I'll send you an e-mail or a letter.'" His take is that people were evenly divided, pro Wailea 670 or con.

"When everything was said and done, I believe Wailea 670 will be good for Maui County, because 250 affordable housing units would have to be built first."

In the past, he said, we have been "cheated" (he used a less charitable word) too many times. "We worked on (Wailea 670) for one year, and it started 20 years ago. In my deliberations, sometimes I wasn't sure. But the bottom line is, for every major project that comes up in the future, the template has been set," he explained.

In addition, he noted, the development firm did not get a free hand. "We set 44 conditions. Now you've got to put in affordable housing up front," he said.

In considering future development, Victorino insists the council needs to pay great attention to density. He has no problem with newcomers' desire to live on Maui.

"I really believe affordable housing is first and foremost. But in my heart, if a fat cat wants to come here and build a beautiful house, and that house will generate taxes and other revenue streams, there is nothing wrong with that. This is America. But the working people, the people who live here, who want to stay here, should have the first choice," he said.

Victorino also does not think much of the idea that developers should be required to build only affordable housing. The county would be sued over that issue, he claimed.

As decisions on development or limited development continue, Victorino said he will look for guidance from the county's new General Plan. Although some might say Victorino deserves a Valentine for supporting affordable housing, others sharply differ.

Approximately 250 of 700 affordable units are in a Kihei industrial zone that could be regarded as less than desirable. If the county is so intent on affordable housing, why not develop a plan and ask developers to bid on it?

Why can't the county simply reject a project, instead of trying to find a compromise – give us this, we will give you that.

And where else do you find developers so thankful to county officials that they feel compelled to run gushy, thank you radio advertisements?

October 16, 2008

Postscript: Victonino has consistently voted with pro-development forces the last few years. Meanwhile, the much fought over Makena project has been delayed as the result of a financing foreclosure.

NIKHILANANDA
Talk Show Host

Voting for aunties and uncles doesn't make for good government

There will be a new cast of characters in the debating society over in Wailuku otherwise known as the County Council that helps govern all of Maui County. The society talks and talks, but to many, rarely appears to get anything done. Perhaps it is time to adopt the popular political expression, "Throw the rascals out."

For advice, we turned to Nick Nikhilananda, one of the most world-wise (50 states, 50 countries visited) and knowledgeable observers of the Maui scene we know. "Nicky" isn't endorsing anyone, with the possible exception of West Maui Council incumbent Jo Anne Johnson.

"Our local elections are still very provincial," he insists. "People still vote for their aunties, uncles, cousins or somebody because their daddy was on the council. We just don't get a real cross-section of people. And they owe a lot of their power to some of the large developers, the old-time landowners or new ones," he explained.

Council members say they care about the community, Nicky continued, "But when it comes to affordable housing, they approve a high-end gated community in South Maui while they could use the same time to say yes to affordable housing. The way we do development? Backwards. Someone comes in and says, 'I want to do this,' but it does not fit the county plan. They give them variances. (The council) talks about affordable housing but has done next to nothing. They give lip service to what the people want."

"High-end developments sell out right away," he added. "People resent (newcomers) who buy these high-end houses and we lose more access to beaches. This creates a tension in the community."

Nikhilananda said that when there is public testimony on these issues, "you are given three minutes, but someone with a big development can have hours with their glossy photos and power point presentations, and they can respond to any criticism."

Among the few positives he cites coming from the council the last few years is support for the highly successful Maui bus system, plus the work of Councilwoman Michelle Anderson, who is NOT running for reelection. He praised her for taking on major issues, including water, and for her passion and caring attitude toward the community.

The main local government failures, according to Nikhilananda, are lack of responsiveness to the community, a poor record in actually getting affordable housing built, not dealing with traffic issues, not preserving open space and access to beaches, and not dealing with the high cost of living, which forces residents to work multiple jobs.

So what can be done? Nikhilananda, who first stepped in Maui in 1978 and has lived here for 22 years, admits to being cynical. He feels it's very important to speak out and tell it like it is, because so few do.

He would like to see council members elected by State Senate district in their own area. All voters now vote for all members, whether they represent Kahului, Lahaina, Upcountry or even Lana'i and Moloka'i. He is pessimistic, believing those elected through this system don't want to change it.

Disappointed with some candidates elected last term for failing to live up to their potential, Nikhilananda said everyone running for reelection, except Johnson, should be defeated. He wants well-educated people of intelligence and vision on the council, with the ability to think creatively to meet the challenges. It's up to the voters to figure out which candidates qualify, he said.

If he could wave a magic wand, he would institute campaign finance reform, change to district voting, allow write-in voting, spend more money on public transportation, increase taxes for affluent home buyers, encourage local farming, start curbside recycling, promote renewable energy and have a state constitutional convention to strip the state of some of its responsibilities and give them to the county.

Nikhilananda sounds like a guy who ought to be elected. Unfortunately, he has tried more than once and lost. This year he is not on the ballot. Maybe it was just that most people either weren't listening or weren't voting. Think about it. And vote on Sept. 20.

September 4, 2008

Postscript: Nikhilananda continues his long-running community access TV show called Maui Talks TV. Almost all the candidates he favored for election lost.

DIANE PURE
Volunteer

Pure enthusiasm, all for community

At Opportunity Rocks, an event created by Diane Pure, eighth graders at Lahaina Intermediate School, ham it up for the camera before start of the morning Opportunity Rocks session on career possibilities at hotels.

Knowing Diane (Sawyer) Pure, a writer is reminded of advertising slogans. First, she's like Ivory soap, "99.44 percent pure"—Pure enthusiasm, Pure community commitment. Second she is like the energizer bunny, going and going, giving and giving.

How Massachusetts-born Diane wound up on Maui isn't too much different from the experience of many newcomers. Yet, unlike some who buy homes here but mostly take up space and live like they did back home, Diane rates an A-plus.

Diane reports that coming to Maui for the first time "we felt like country bumpkins," Diane said. "We walked through the Hyatt (lobby), looked up to the ceiling and found out there was none. We had been fighting foul weather all our lives." Bob said, "We are going to make a pact. We are going to come here every year."

In 2000, the Pures received an offer they could not refuse from a French company bent on expansion. They sold their three-location bed accessory store and when no new opportunity opened up they said to themselves, "Let's do it."

"We just decided we had had one cloudburst and rainstorm too many." Pulling up stakes they purchased a two-bedroom condo in Ka'anapali for a permanent residence.

Daughter of a military careerist, Diane lived in 15 different towns growing up, spending three years in Berlin, Germany in high school. She starred in college at the University of Connecticut, securing a business degree (as one of only 25 women in a class of 1200 men.)

Diane Sawyer met and married Bob when both held managerial positions at the specialty store, Filene's of Boston. When kids came along, she decided to stay home because she wanted to give them the stability she lacked growing up. Bob became a crackerjack purchasing/merchandising executive working for Gimbels in New York and Philadelphia while living in New Jersey.

Along the way, there was always community involvement, second nature to Diane. Military families who move a lot have a tradition of volunteering to quickly make friends in new communities, she said. Diane showed early spark by organizing a successful effort to toss corrupt officials out of office and invariably found herself becoming president of almost ever organization she joined.

On Maui, she linked up with Richard and Pat Endsley's highly praised tutoring program. From there, it was a short step to launching two unique special projects.

These days, the ability of seniors to win scholarships or win the coveted prizes. Students are taught to write good personal statements essential to getting grants and are prepped for scholarship interviews so they can wow decision makers.

Putting to work her personnel skills as an experienced interviewer and judge of people, she interviews each student for 30 minutes and spends another hour with them reviewing their first drafts.

Some students are asked to redo their statements as many as six times. Scheduled follow-up phone calls complete the process. At least 15 hours a week go into the effort. The payoff: her charges won $188,000 in scholarships and financial aid last year.

Diane's latest initiative was creating and organizing "Opportunity Rocks," a year in planning.

Pure discovered that most eighth graders do not have a clue about what is involved in preparing for careers and what opportunities there are in the island's biggest industry—tourism.

Pure lined up five hotels–Hyatt Regency Resort and Spa, Ka'anapali Beach Hotel, Lahaina Royal, Westin, and the Ritz Carlton, Kapalua—to put on morning-long programs on career opportunities for 250 eighth graders at Lahaina Intermediate School.

She also recruited 50 chaperones from all walks of life to accompany them. Opportunity Rocks won heavy praise from all participants and the hotels stepped up big time.

Diane soldiers on, sold on the value of contributing to the community.

November 4, 2008

Final Voices:
Newcomers/Kupuna

NORM BEZANE
Lahaina News Columnist

A nostalgic look at 27 years as a visitor

*Author and son Conor in 1991, before the parent took up residency
10 years later.*

Mainlanders often fondly remember summers at the lake. Our
family waxes nostalgic about decades of vacationing on Maui before we,
as parents became permanent residents in 2001. This reminisce, taking a
look back at the ever-changing Maui seen as experienced from a visitor's

perspective, offers a glimpse of how Maui has changed, and how, in some respects, it remains the same.

Thirty years ago, when the world famous Ka'anapali Beach Resort was a one-time dream destination for legions of bubbly honeymooners and visitors on seven-day package tours, those with that first time in paradise glow didn't think much about coming back. Our kids were an exception, returning on vacation with us nearly 27 different years in the seventies, eighties, and nineties.

They stepped foot on Maui for the first time on Hawaiian Airlines planes that then debarked people right on the tarmac before there were jet ways. Over the years they rode in "umbrella" strollers, toddled across rope bridges, sailed on catamarans and floated over Ka'anapali on a parasail, as they grew older, finally returning as adults arrive at fairly cosmopolitan Kahului Airport.

In those early years, you hopped on Hawaiian Air on Oahu after a trip from the mainland and deplaned to walk to a sleepy baggage claim area, picking up your bags near a tall tree that stood in the center of the terminal.

Today, from our bulging photo album, spring forth not only our "Ka'anapali Kids" but the remarkable evolution of one of the world's best-planned and workable resorts—a resort that no longer is the exclusive paradise for just newlyweds and first time tourists.

Now, as the ads say, the world comes to play, and Ka'anapali Kids once so rare can now be found on every beach and around every corner, many on return trips.

Paging through the family album not only brings back memories of the seventies, eighties and nineties on Ka'anapali: it brings the realization that we have more photos of our kids two-week sojourns to Ka'anapali (often each Easter) than from the 50 weeks we spent annually at home in Chicago.

There are even some from Honolulu, including one memorable frame taken when an entertainer we remember as "Sonia" picked her up and sang to her at the old Garden Bar at Hilton Hawaiian Village.

The first night away from home with our six-month-old daughter was spent at the Kahana Sunset even before there was a Kapalua just up the road. Evenings were enjoyed in Ka'anapali or Lahaina, with our daughter frequently tucked in a stroller sleeping under a restaurant table somewhere while we dined on ahi or filet mignon.

Given our daughter's continuing ability to fall asleep easily anywhere, we used to say that our young traveler had slept at all the best restaurants in

Lahaina, including Kimos and even outside the fancier Longhi's Restaurant, parked on the sidewalk below an open window. We dined just inside to the amusement —in those days—of not so-frequent passersby.

Though we are still lean people, a lot of the photos and memories revolve around eating. At our usual 5 a.m. jet-lagged awakening on a first day in Maui, we evolved a tradition of driving to the Hyatt (then called a hotel and not a resort) for an early walk through the Japanese garden.

This would be followed by pineapple pancakes in Lahaina Town at historic Pioneer Inn overlooking the harbor. Once or twice a trip we would return, broiling our own dinners you could cook yourself in the interior courtyard (mahi, seven minutes). The cook-your-own barbecue pit is no more, as are most of the hundreds of whaling artifacts on the wall of the bar within view of a fleet of fishing boats. Now only a few remain.

The broil-your-own concept was also a staple at the Old Rusty Harpoon, since reinvented as the only true sports bar on Ka'anapali Beach, now recently moved to a new location near the entrance to Ka'anapali (another change).

We'd grill our own burgers—some of the best we've ever tasted—against a backdrop of fresh sea air and Moloka'i in the distance.

Another favorite spot was the old Crab Catcher restaurant, predecessor to today's popular Hula Grill at Whalers Village Shopping Center, centerpiece of the resort area right on the ocean.

Besides scrumptious nachos unlike any to be found today—so it seems—the Crab Catcher featured a small swimming pool where our kids could wade or swim while we ate hamburgers (we both still ate meat and had better teeth in those days). Also remembered fondly was the once-nearby Chicos, the place for tacos before anyone had ever heard of one of today's island favorites, Maui Tacos.

It was at Whalers Village that I once left our newborn son in a stroller in the aisle of the old bookstore next to Rusty Harpoon, only to leave and then remember that we had had a second child and he had been left behind. (He was still there, fast asleep alongside the Hawaiana book section).

And then there were visits to Yami Yogurt that was so good we wished we could get it in Chicago and nearby Riccos, the cozy open air pizza place where a "new" air conditioned fast food court now stands. Both have been casualties of progress.

Our Ka'anapali Kids did more than eat and stay on the beach. We'd go to the community Easter Egg hunt under the Banyan Tree in town each year, with our son one time finding the golden egg entitling him to special prize, a canister of Play Doh. And of course there was Easter egg coloring at three different resorts and the Makawao Rodeo on Fourth of July.

There were family milestones too. One life-changing event occurred on the curving golf course lined pathway along Ka'anapali Parkway one evening in 1981. My wife Sara and I made a life-changing decision that one of us would quit work.

In the days when it was rare for husband and wife to both have demanding careers with two kids; it was along Ka'anapali Parkway that I decided to quit my job as a corporate publications manager and stay home as one of the earliest househusbands.

Today, passing by now almost daily, I remember the walkway fondly since the decision there, it turned out, was one of the most rewarding ones I have ever made.

One blustery day on our 23rd trip, tragedy almost struck. In a first and only use of a video camera, I decided to film an entire day of our favorite family activities, mynas chirping at wakeup, breakfast at Pioneer Inn, a ride on the Ka'anapali resort trolley and a day at the beach.

Author's wife Sara, who first set foot in Maui in 1969, and grownup daughter Foley who has visited paradise nearly two dozen times since she was six months old. Foley, our Ka'anapali Kid whose first name is the same as her mother Sara's maiden name, enjoys her 24th visit to Maui since she first came here as an infant.

Videotaping away, I was glad to see the enormous and picturesque waves that wife and kids plunged into for "the ocean shot." Problem was my wife got in trouble, saved only by the fact that our daughter had become a good swimmer. Our 34-year old refuses to look at the video to this day.

Our Ka'anapali Kids are no longer kids now but they still keep coming back from Chicago and New York to what we sometimes called "Conorpali Beach. We used to say to our young son Conor that one day he would own one of the houses behind the colorful rows of azaleas facing Honoapiilani Highway in front of Ka'anapali Beach Resort.

He doesn't own one yet but you never know. But his Ka'anapali parents now own a permanent residence close by, down the hill from Ka'anapali not far away. Since 2001, we've learned that living on Maui is far different than visiting.

We came from a big city, and this is a small town. One of us—not me—thought we'd get "island fever," a fear that a small island would not be enough to keep us happy and busy. Alas, we have found that music is everywhere, almost every weekend brings a festival and the days are so packed with work or community related activities visits to the beach become rarer and rarer.

Years ago, in the Midwest, family memories of many people used to revolve around summers at the lake. Ours are filled with fond memories of Ka'anapali Beach and Lahaina, as they will in the years ahead for increasing numbers of Ka'anapali Kids building new traditions on the greatest place on earth. Maybe some will even wind up living in paradise, becoming Voices of Maui too.

BARBARA SHARP
History Buff

Keeping a Sharp eye on our heritage

Reverend Dwight Baldwin and wife Charlotte– portrayed in a 2009 Progressive Dinner event at historical venues. The missionaries must have stood in this precise spot during the whaling era. Pioneer Inn in front of them was not built until 1901.

Missionaries and whaling captains again in the news (because of the Lahaina Restoration Foundation Progressive Dinner staged to portray these first non-natives at four historic venues preserved for future generations) are a reminder that the lives of these New England wayfarers remain as interesting today as they were 150 years ago.

Just ask Barbara Sharp, who for ten years served as research director of the foundation and penned a Lahaina mystery series. Sharp performed the feat of transcribing 3,000 pages of historical documents gathered together as the Windley Files. A better name might now be the Windley/Sharp Files.

Windley, recovering from a diving accident in the 1950s that left him paralyzed for a time and later unable to pursue his passion for ocean depths, recruited a team to go to Oahu to visit history repositories. The group copied on small cards hundreds and hundreds of passages from logs, letters, journals and first person accounts of what life was like in Lahaina in the 1800s.

Years later, Sharp — new on Maui and answering an ad to transcribe old microfilm records for Lahaina Restoration Foundation — soon found herself capturing tens of thousands of words from deteriorating Windley carbon copies and putting them on a computer. The task took three years, and the result is a printout of 13 books up to 400 pages long.

Reading just a few of the Windley pages, a fascinating and colorful picture emerges of Old Lahaina. Reverend and physician Dwight Baldwin, the most prominent of the missionaries who made his home here from 1834-68, during those years saw Lahaina flourish and then begin to decline.

Most whaling ships manned by 25 sailors would spend two weeks in Lahaina for new provisions and "R&R." Lahaina was filled with wall-to-wall people at night, just like today, with whalers ferried to town in shifts to get drunk on rum and local beer made from potatoes. Soap was added to make the beer foam, leaving imbibers with powerful headaches.

Meanwhile, the missionaries were continually pushing for prohibition. Captains, a more mature lot who tended to be religious, often spent their time in the Masters Reading Room scanning six-month-old newspapers.

In 1843, Lahaina boasted three chandlery shops to supply 96 whaling ships in port, 15 retailers, three doctors and the new Lahainaluna Seminary.

By 1859, a bowling alley, seven eatery houses, six sly drinking establishments and one billiard room had been added. More than 100 ships arrived that year, down from a peak of 393 in 1856. The heyday of whaling was soon over, transforming the town into "a dirty and dilapidated village" by the 1870s, according to one account.

Early on, Baldwin firmly opposed foreigner's participation in local government, telling Hawaiians prophetically, "you better watch out for your sovereignty." Wearing many hats, Rev. Baldwin practiced medicine here and on Moloka'i and Lana'i, and by 1860 was preaching to crowds of 2,300 people (100 foreigners and 2,500 Hawaiians lived in Lahaina at the time).

"People think the missionaries were anti-hula and anti-everything," according to Sharp. The truth is they learned the Hawaiian language on the ships that brought them here and loved Hawaiians. They worked with people like Hawaiian scholar David Malo to write down history.

"For 50 years," Sharp noted, "Hawaiian was the language in the schools and church and was used in all the publications. Once they stopped speaking Hawaiian in the schools, they went downhill."

Locals portrayed missionaries Dwight and Charlott Baldwin and their daughters during a 2009 Progressive dinner event celebration sponsored by the Lahaina Restoration Foundation.

Sharp credits the missionaries for writing down the language phonetically to perpetuate it.

With missionaries and Hawaiians, "it was mutual love." One Hawaiian even requested burial next to his missionary friend, after they became buddies through their common interest in astronomy.

The New Englanders viewed Maui like most of the rest of us. They fell in love with island beauty. "They didn't have to stay here all their lives; it wasn't a jail sentence. They could have gone home but they didn't want to leave. They were not necessarily all religious. Some went on to become businessmen, some good, some bad. This became their home," Sharp noted.

The Windley Files transcriber has self-published six "Lahaina Mysteries" with numerous passages providing historically accurate tales of older times. More than 7,000 copies of her books — sold only at Buns of Maui, the Lahaina Visitor Center and Village Gallery — are now in print. A seventh mystery is due by Christmas.

The main character in the series is a cat-loving historian — actually a thinly disguised Sharp. Both grew up in Seattle and had gourmet coffee shops there.

The mystery writer's only lament these days is how Lahaina has changed. She used to find peaceful inspiration along the seawall on Front Street, where she said she would "go into a Zen-like state" and find new ideas for her books. "Now noisy leaf blowers have taken over," she complained.

Sharp never set out to be a writer, yet finds writing surprisingly easy. Her greatest contribution, however, may not be in her books, but in her dedicated work preserving the Windley Files. Windley died at a young age, but thanks to Barbara Sharp, his legacy lives on.

HELEN REED
Food Critic/Retiree

Irrepressible sailor becomes champagne sipping "Maui girl"

Some people live a charmed life. The irrepressible 84- years-young Helen Reed, Lahaina News food critic for the last 12 years, is one. And like many, she's found a new life in paradise after an equally lively one on and off the mainland.

At ages three, five and 14 in Los Angeles, she was hit by automobiles and survived. At 60, the big "C" entered her lithe body. She had a breast removed and survived. Still later, colon cancer arrived. Helen survived that, too. Today she still thrives and wants to live to be 100 or more.

If the life of willowy, muscular Helen Reed was summed up in a want ad, it would read:

WANTED

Gourmet cook, superb freelance writer (200 articles for the Los Angeles Times syndicate, The Maui News, Yachting magazine and this newspaper), author of a forthcoming memoir, world traveler to seven continents, Rotarian, devoted wife of 47 years.

More than anything, the irrepressible Helen is an adventuress – a trait picked up from her New York-born mom. At 37, Helen married string bass player Rob Reed, musician for Disney's Mickey Mouse Club and performer on the popular commercial "See the USA in Your Chevrolet." The two soon set out to pursue their love of the sea.

They bought a 65-foot ketch sailing boat and refitted it to accommodate ten paying guests. Helen realized her dream of cooking gourmet food on the for-charter yacht, and Rob served as captain. Helen calculated that she has served up more than 16,000 gourmet meals over ten years to weekly guests, including on one New Year's Eve legendary newsman (and sailor) Walter Cronkite and family.

The Reeds worked out of St. Thomas, living on the boat and cruising 12 Caribbean islands. Their summers were spent traveling the U.S. in a Winnebago until 1983, when Helen was diagnosed with cancer. Recouping from the operation at a friend's home on Maui, they spotted a pole house with an unbelievable view of the ocean above Kahana and bought it on the spot. They have lived there ever since.

Life on Maui has included community involvement — helping to get a fire station in Napili and serving as an inspiration to cancer survivors as an active member of the West Maui Relay for Life. In the '90s, Helen and Rob traveled to what appears to be nearly every exotic spot on Earth, including Russia, China, Egypt, Kenya, and even around the horn through the Straits of Magellan to Antarctica.

Back home, wanting to share her experiences, she would always plug in her trusty Smith Corona electric typewriter and begin pounding away. She is now writing memoirs titled "Treasurers of the Thirties."

Reading a handful of clippings Reed provided, it is clear if she is as good a cook as she is a writer, she would be in the same league as the best chefs on Maui. Maui chefs, in fact, are the equal of the best anywhere in the world, she said.

Reed nevertheless has a gift. She has written equally telling tales of riding through two hurricanes in one week on her boat (winds up to 120 mph), and stories about the cuisine she has sampled everywhere she has gone.

Helen's solid reputation as a food writer got her named "de la Chaine des Rotisseurs" in the international society of cuisine that is very picky about who can join. She's been greeted with respect and with culinary treats by chefs from the Tavern on the Green in New York to a galley on a Russian cruise ship. She has feasted on coconut bread and parrot fish in Fiji, Dover sole in London, cottage cheese egg pudding in Russia, the meat of wildebeest in Kenya and other fare, in places from the San Blas Islands near Panama to ships going through the Suez Canal.

Describing herself as "a Maui girl," Reed is rarely seen without her thong slippers. Delighted with snowflakes beating down near the coast of Antarctica alongside glaciers ten stories high, she once stepped on the deck in bare feet nestled in thongs, while her fellow passengers were bundled in boots and parkas.

One of the unique things about Maui is that it often attracts the best of the best. Helen is right up there. Her zest for life holds no bounds, leading this daughter of a milkman — who knows of the Great Depression — to be willing to freely spend the hard-earned money she and Rob earned from their charter business.

"I encourage everyone to seek all the adventure you can," she explained. "Life is too short to not live it fully. We can't waste one moment of our Earth time. Remember, if we don't go first-class, our heirs will," she has told her husband.

With this outlook, she places a big premium on being fit. "I lift weights three times a week," she said, exhibiting building arm muscles. "I do at least 240 lifts each time because Papa (the affectionate name she calls her husband) has good life span in his family. I don't have that much, so I have to stay around and take care of him."

Reed appears to be disappointed in just one thing: what is happening on Maui. "It's becoming another Waikiki. This is just not right," she said.

Around Maui, Reed is known as the Champagne Lady, serving it at the many parties on Maui she's hosted and quaffing it on her many travels. She even offered a glass to this columnist one recent morning. A toast definitely would have been in order: To you, irrepressible Helen.

NA KUPUNA AND OTHERS

Maui at the crossroads

Kupuna, musicians, cultural advisors, island icons, elected officials, community leaders, and business people have all spoken out on these pages. Some of their words are worth repeating. And some, equally enlightened, are new.

With this island at a crossroads — Superferry, vacation rentals, Honolua Bay, Wailea 670, development or no development, affordable housing or luxury housing, preservation of aloha spirit and cultural values or destruction of those values, preservation of taro patches or road construction — what we need more than anything is wisdom. Those in a position of power need to take seriously the letters they read each morning in the papers or the testimony they hear at midnight hearings (yes we had one) and act accordingly.

Community volunteer: "We thought we moved to Maui for the beauty. It turns out we moved here for the beautiful people." (Paraphrase, 8/31/07)

Hinano Rodrigues of Olowalu: "Stopping development is like trying to blot out the sun. It is not an alternative. It is not going to happen. We live in a capitalistic world. Capitalism snowballs. You cannot stop it. What we need to do is have controlled development. We need to find a balance? I truly believe we should permit development only when developers can prove that they have water. Water is a limited resource on this island." (8/2/07)

Community leader: "It was a brilliant idea 30 years ago and it's a brilliant idea today. But nobody paid attention." (9/5/07, paraphrased)

Jamie DeBrunner, Old Lahaina Luau: "People traveled thousands of miles and have been sold a commercial image of Hawaii. But now you know that we are so much more than hula girls and swaying palms and sunsets.

We look to the mountains and we look to the sea. And you see so much more than you have ever seen before." (10/26/06)

Tony Vericella, event planner: "We have something that is so special and unique that nobody has, and we need to share it in the right way, not give it away to chase the almighty dollar that sometimes people get caught up in." (10/26/07)

Resident: "Don't make Hawaiian culture parsley on the plate. Make it the meat and potatoes." (General lanning meeting, 7/08)

Brent Schlea, resident: "We need to stop the tide of commercial development, which creates an ever-increasing spiral of municipal costs. Once we decide that our surroundings need not always be subordinated to payrolls and profits, based on short-term considerations, there is hope. The most valuable use for the land is to leave it as it stands, preserved for future generations to enjoy." (5/3/07)

Doug Pitzer, contractor: "We need a building moratorium; we need it now." (5/3/07)

Clifford Nae'ole, cultural advisor: "If you were born here and choose to live here, you are part of the solution. If you are living in a gated community, the question is, are you keeping people out, or are you keeping yourself in? You worked hard and you deserve what you have, but don't lock yourself out." (4/5/07)

Councilwoman Jo Anne Johnson: "Which is better for your constituents: siding with that loyalty, that old line company; or siding with doing the right things for the right reasons. I am hoping the new council members will ignore these ties. Their kids are going to have to live with whatever is done." (1/25/07)

Councilwomen Jo Anne Johnson: "We must look forward seven generations. This is a Hawaiian concept. If we do not do projects and land use planning that is pono (right and good), I believe we will ultimately fail in our efforts. To do things in the proper way, we need to act with respect for the host culture in all endeavors." (2/08/07)

ANDREA RAZZAUTI
Artist/Musician

Is art music or music art?

Artist/Musician Andrea Razzauti (right) chats with Lahaina Galleries owner Jim Killett who is portrayed in a previous section on "Movers and Shakers." One of the artist's classic paintings celebrating sand beaches and seascapes is in the background.

Strolling down picturesque Front Street, Andrea Razzauti of Tuscany, Italy in 1999 headed through the door of Lahaina Galleries, one of the state's most prestigious purveyors of art. Andrea was a man of few words that day. He only knew a few English phrases.

"I am an artist, this is my book (of samples)." This he said to the first person he encountered. The art consultant had probably heard this claim hundreds of times. The work that Andrea had been preparing for almost a year on the islands spoke for itself.

Andrea Razzauti, a well-known artist in his native Italy, was now on his way to becoming equally as known in the United States. Andrea's paintings would be displayed in a new venue.

Razzauti is not the first artist from far away places to find a home on Maui, attracted as they have been by the fabulous light and beauty of the island and its people. He joined a kind of 'ohana of nearly a dozen artists from different countries who live or frequently have painted in Hawaii and whose work is exhibited at Jim Killett's Lahaina Galleries.

When Razzauti appears at a Friday Art Night, he is sometimes joined by Italian natives Dario Campanille and the twin brothers Allesio and Marcello Bugagiare who paint often on Hawaiian koa wood. Then there's Brazil-born Ronaldo Marcedo, lured here by the surfing who stayed to paint and raise a family.

Razzauti at his core is a super perfectionist among his perfectionist colleagues. Today he has a strong sense of what a painting should be and also, amazingly, how a musical composition should be crafted.
To Andrea Razzauti, art is music and music is art.

As a small boy, Andrea was fortunate to have had a perfect role model, his father, Ivo, a well-known artist who was also an accomplished musician. His mother, Emilia, was a musician as well. Inspired by the masters whose works he saw every day, with playmates who were the sons and daughters of artists, there could have been no other calling for Andrea than art and music.

Razzauti was also surrounded by some of the Italian masters of the day, including French impressionists, futuristic cubists and abstractionists. Older artists who were his contemporaries frequently conversed with him about the history and meaning of art and how to visualize a subject on canvas.
By 16, Andrea had his first show.

Thirty-six shows in the finest galleries in Italy, France, Germany, England and Japan followed over the next 28 years. And then 22 more shows the last 10 years in the U.S.A.

Even earlier, at 14, Andrea was playing music for popular bands, eventually winning acclaim over the years playing a variety of styles from traditional classic to R and B to rock and roll. In 1980, he saw the affinity between the classical and the jazz guitar and successfully combined the two.

In 1990, he composed and produced his first album blending classical, Brazilian, and jazz. More recently, Andrea has grown even more intensely passionate about music, still painting every day but also practicing hard daily and composing as well.

As Razzauti composes, he sees himself "completing a musical picture." When Grammy-award-winning producer and guitarist Paul Brown heard Razzauti play some of his compositions on guitar, he immediately said, 'let's make an album. This is great.' Razzauti recorded with the legendary jazz singer Patti Austin and is now working on a second album with her.

For 37 years, Andrea has been on an artistic quest, forever striving to evolve and achieve what he describes as achieve "technical and meaningful soulful perfection."

During his daily pursuit, the prolific artist of landscapes, seascapes and still life follows a mantra that can be summed up in the words of another transplanted European, the late great architect Mies van der Rohe of Chicago. It was Mies who said: "less is more." Andrea says when I compose music I see the pictures. When I am by the easel I paint the music.

More is more. Less is more in the depiction of a white sand beach, fragrand lavendar field, shimmering sea or the essential melodies of his musical compositions. Spare the details. Since the 1960's, Maui has become a mecca for visitors. Now it is a mecca for artists as well.

Written, July 2008, as introduction to the book, "Art is Music, Music is Art."

Postscript: Until recent times, many talented artists who have settled on Maui have prospered, inspired by their surroundings while making a decent style of living in a high cost state. During these recessionary times, artists are not exactly starving—it says here—but harder days are upon them. Razzauti has moved back to an earlier abode he owns in Hilo, Hawaii and has just release a new jazz album, "Painting with Music."

Epilogue

A PRESIDENT
AND A HAWAIIAN PEAR

(In a letter to the United States Congress in 1893, President Grover Cleveland declared that the overthrow of the Hawaiian government and Queen Lili'uokalani represented "an act of war," in which a "friendly and confiding people" and "the lawful Government of Hawaii was overthrown without the drawing of a sword or the firing of a shot by a process.... wholly without justification."

This readable account presents a clear picture of events culminating in the formation of a U.S. territory, and its successor, the State of Hawaii. Hawaiian sovereignty advocates base much of their case on what happened during these fateful days.

"**The ownership of Hawaii was tendered to us** by a provisional government set up to succeed the constitutional ruler of the islands, who had been dethroned.... **It did not appear that such provisional government had the sanction of either popular revolution or suffrage.** Two other remarkable features of the transaction naturally attracted attention.

"...One was **the extraordinary haste**—not to say precipitancy— characterizing all the transactions connected with it. It appeared that a so-called Committee of Safety, ostensibly the source of the revolt against the constitutional Government of Hawaii, was organized on Saturday, the 14th day of January; that on Monday, the 16th, the United States forces were landed at Honolulu from a naval vessel lying in its harbor...

"...On the 17th the scheme of a provisional government was perfected, and a proclamation naming its officers was on the same day prepared and read at the Government building; that immediately thereupon the United States Minister recognized the provisional government thus created; that two days afterwards, on the 19th day of January, commissioners representing such government sailed for this country in a steamer especially chartered for the occasion, arriving in San Francisco on the 28th day of January.

"...In Washington on the 3rd day of February they had their first interview with the Secretary of State, and another on the 11th, when the treaty of annexation was practically agreed upon, and that on the 14th it was formally concluded and on the 15th transmitted to the Senate.

"Thus between the initiation of the scheme for a provisional government in Hawaii on the 14th day of January and the submission to the Senate of the treaty of annexation concluded with such government, the entire interval was thirty-two days, fifteen of which were spent by the Hawaiian Commissioners in their journey to Washington...

"The message of the President accompanying the treaty declared that 'the overthrow of the monarchy was not in any way promoted by this Government'...

"At the time the provisional government took possession of the Government buildings no troops or officers of the United States were present or took any part whatever in the proceedings. No public recognition was accorded to the provisional government by the United States Minister until after the Queen's abdication and when they were in effective possession of the Government buildings, the archives, the treasury, the barracks, the police station, and all the potential machinery of the Government.

"But a protest also accompanied said treaty, signed by the Queen and her ministers at the time she made way for the provisional government, which explicitly stated that **she yielded to the superior force of the United States, whose Minister had caused United States troops to be landed at Honolulu and declared that he would support such provisional government**. The truth or falsity of this protest was surely of the first importance.

"...A treaty resulting from the acts stated in the protest have been knowingly deemed worthy of consideration by the Senate. Yet the truth or falsity of the protest had not been investigated. **I conceived it to be my duty therefore to withdraw the treaty from the Senate for examination**....

"On the 19th day of November, 1892, nearly two months before the first overt act tending towards the subversion of the Hawaiian Government and the attempted transfer of Hawaiian territory to the United States, (the U.S representative) addressed a long letter to the Secretary of State...(in which) he refers to the loss of the Hawaiian sugar interests from the operation of the McKinley bill, and the tendency to still further depreciation of sugar property unless some positive measure of relief is granted.

"He strongly inveighs against the existing Hawaiian Government and emphatically declares for annexation. He says: **"In truth the monarchy here is an absurd anachronism. It has nothing on which it logically or legitimately stands. The feudal basis on which it once stood no longer existing, the monarchy now is only an impediment to good government - an obstruction to the prosperity and progress of the islands."**...

"Hawaii has reached the parting of the ways. She must now take the road which leads to Asia, or the other which outlets her in America, gives her an American civilization, and binds her to the care of American destiny." He also declares: "One of two courses seems to me absolutely necessary to be followed, either bold and vigorous measures for annexation or a 'customs union," an ocean cable from the Californian coast to Honolulu, Pearl Harbor perpetually ceded to the United States, with an implied but not expressly stipulated American protectorate over the islands....

"To a minister of this temper full of zeal for annexation there seemed to arise in January, 1893, the precise opportunity for which he was watchfully waiting... an opportunity which by timely "deviation from established international rules and precedents" might be improved to successfully accomplish the great object in view; and we are quite prepared for the exultant enthusiasm with which in a letter to the State Department dated February 1, 1893, he declares: **'The Hawaiian pear is now fully ripe and this is the golden hour for the United States to pluck it.'"**

"...he (then) issued a proclamation whereby "in the name of the United States" he assumed the protection of the Hawaiian Islands and declared that said action was "taken pending and subject to negotiations at Washington."....

"On Saturday, January 14, 1893, the Queen of Hawaii, who had been contemplating the proclamation of a new constitution, had, in deference to the wishes and remonstrances of her cabinet, renounced the project for the present at least. Taking this relinquished purpose as a basis of action, citizens of Honolulu numbering from fifty to one hundred, mostly resident aliens, met in a private office and selected a so-called Committee of Safety, composed of thirteen persons, seven of whom were foreign subjects, and consisted of five Americans, one Englishman, and one German....

"On Monday morning the Queen and her cabinet made public proclamation, with a notice which was specially served upon the representatives of all foreign governments, that any changes in the constitution would be sought only in the methods provided by that instrument.

"Nevertheless, at the call and under the auspices of the Committee of Safety, **a mass meeting of citizens was held on that day to protest against the Queen's alleged illegal and unlawful proceedings and purposes**. Even at this meeting the Committee of Safety ...denouncing the Queen and empowering the committee to devise ways and means "to secure the permanent maintenance of law and order and the protection of life, liberty, and property in Hawaii...

"On the same day... the committee, unwilling to take further steps without the cooperation of the United States Minister, addressed him a note representing that the public safety was menaced and that lives and property were in danger, and concluded as follows:

"**We are unable to protect ourselves without aid, and therefore pray for the protection of the United States forces.**" "... The committee, so far as it appears, had neither a man or a gun at their command,...

they became so panic-stricken at their stricken position that they sent some of their number to... request him not to land the United States forces till the next morning.... on the 16th day of January, 1893, between four and five o'clock in the afternoon, a detachment of marines from the United States Steamer Boston, with two pieces of artillery, landed at Honolulu.

"The men, upwards of 160 in all, were supplied with double cartridge belts filled with ammunition and with haversacks and canteens, and were accompanied by a hospital corps with stretchers and medical supplies. This military demonstration upon the soil of Honolulu was of itself an act of war, unless made either with the consent of the Government of Hawaii or for the bona fide purpose of protecting the imperiled lives and property of citizens of the United States.

"But there is no pretense of any such consent on the part of the Government of the Queen, which at that time was undisputed and was both the de facto and the de jure government. In point of fact the existing government instead of requesting the presence of an armed force protested....

"When these armed men were landed, the city of Honolulu was in its customary orderly and peaceful condition. There was no symptom of riot or disturbance in any quarter. Men, women, and children were about the streets as usual, and nothing varied the ordinary routine or disturbed the ordinary tranquility, except the landing of the Boston's marines and their march through the town to the quarters assigned them.

"Thus it appears that Hawaii was taken possession of by the United States forces without the consent or wish of the government of the islands, or of anybody else so far as shown, except the United States Minister.

"Therefore he military occupation of Honolulu by the United States on the day mentioned was wholly without justification, either as an occupation by consent or as an occupation necessitated by dangers threatening American life and property. It must be accounted for in some other way and on some other ground, and its real motive and purpose are neither obscure nor far to seek.

"The United States forces being now on the scene and favorably stationed, the committee proceeded to carry out their original scheme. They met the next morning, Tuesday, the 17th, perfected the plan of temporary government, and fixed upon its principal officers, ten of whom were drawn from the thirteen members of the Committee of Safety.

"Between one and two o'clock, by squads and by different routes to avoid notice, and having first taken the precaution of ascertaining whether there was any one there to oppose them, they proceeded to the Government building to proclaim the new government.

"No sign of opposition was manifest, and thereupon an American citizen began to read the proclamation from the steps of the Government building almost entirely without auditors. It is said that before the reading was finished quite a concourse of persons, variously estimated at from 50 to 100, some armed and some unarmed, gathered about the committee to give them aid and confidence.

"The provisional government thus proclaimed was by the terms of the proclamation "to exist until terms of union with the United States had been negotiated and agreed upon". The United States Minister, pursuant to prior agreement, recognized this government within an hour after the reading of the proclamation, and before five o'clock, in answer to an inquiry on behalf of the Queen and her cabinet, announced that he had done so.

"...this wrongful recognition by our Minister placed the Government of the Queen in a position of most perilous perplexity.** On the one hand she had possession of the palace, of the barracks, and of the police station, and had at her command at least five hundred fully armed men and several pieces of artillery. Indeed, the whole military force of her kingdom was on her side and at her disposal, while the Committee of Safety, by actual search, had discovered that there were but very few arms in Honolulu that were not in the service of the Government.

"...(Lili'uokalani) knew that she could not withstand the power of the United States, but she believed that she might safely trust to its justice.** Accordingly, some hours after the recognition of the provisional government by the United States Minister, the palace, the barracks, and the police station, with all the military resources of the country, were delivered up by the Queen upon the representation made to her that her cause would thereafter be reviewed at Washington, and while protesting that **she surrendered to the superior force of the United States**, whose Minister had caused United States troops to be landed at Honolulu and declared that he would support the provisional government, and that **she yielded her authority to prevent collision of armed forces and loss of life and only until such time as the United States, upon the facts being presented to it, should** undo the action of its representative and reinstate her in the authority she claimed as the constitutional sovereign of the Hawaiian Islands.

"...I believe... that the provisional government owes its existence to an armed invasion by the United States. Fair-minded people with the evidence before them will hardly claim that the Hawaiian Government was overthrown by the people of the islands or that the provisional government had ever existed with their consent....

"The lawful Government of Hawaii was overthrown without the drawing of a sword or the firing of a shot by a process every step of which, it may be safely asserted, is directly traceable to and dependent for its success upon the agency of the United States acting through its diplomatic and naval representatives.

But for the notorious predilections of the United States Minister for annexation, the Committee of Safety, which should be called the Committee of Annexation, would "never have existed. But for the landing of the United States forces upon false pretexts respecting the danger to life and property the committee would never have exposed themselves to the pains and penalties of treason by undertaking the subversion of the Queen's Government.

"But for the presence of the United States forces in the immediate vicinity and in position to afford all needed protection and support the committee would not have proclaimed the provisional government from the steps of the Government building.

"And finally, but for the lawless occupation of Honolulu under false pretexts by the United States forces, and but for Minister Stevens' recognition of the provisional government when the United States forces were its sole support and constituted its only military strength, the Queen and her Government would never have yielded to the provisional government, even for a time and for the sole purpose of submitting her case to the enlightened justice of the United States.

"Believing, therefore, that the United States could not, under the circumstances disclosed, annex the islands without justly incurring the imputation of acquiring them by unjustifiable methods, I shall not again submit the treaty of annexation to the Senate for its consideration, and in the instructions to Minister Willis, a copy of which accompanies this message ...it deals. I mistake the American people if they favor the odious doctrine that there is no such thing as international morality, that there is one law for a strong nation and another for a weak one, and that even by indirection a strong power may with impunity despoil a weak one of its territory.

"By an act of war, committed with the participation of a diplomatic representative of the United States and without authority of Congress, the Government of a feeble but friendly and confiding people has been overthrown. A substantial wrong has thus been done which a due regard for our national character as well as the rights of the injured people requires we should endeavor to repair. The provisional government has not assumed a republican or other constitutional form, but has remained a mere executive council or oligarchy, set up without the assent of the people.

"It has not sought to find a permanent basis of popular support and has given no evidence of an intention to do so. Indeed, the representatives of that government assert that the people of Hawaii are unfit for popular government and frankly avow that they can be best ruled by arbitrary or despotic power. ...

"She surrendered not to the provisional government, but to the United States. She surrendered not absolutely and permanently, but temporarily and conditionally until such time as the facts could be considered by the United States....I instructed Minister Willis to advise the Queen and her supporters of my desire to aid in the restoration of the status existing before the lawless landing of the United States forces at Honolulu on the 16th of January last, if such restoration could be effected upon terms providing for clemency as well as justice to all parties concerned. ...I desire to add the assurance that I shall be much gratified to cooperate in any legislative plan which may be devised for the solution of the problem before us which is consistent with American honor, integrity, and morality.

Signed
Grover Cleveland
President of the United States
Executive Mansion,
Washington, December 18, 1893

(Bold face added for emphasis and not in original document)

   Postscript President Cleveland's term expired in 1897. Hawaii was annexed during the administration of President William McKinley in 1898).

THE APOLOGY PUBLIC LAW
103-150

A joint resolution of the 103d Congress
To acknowledge the 100th anniversary of the January 17, 1893 overthrow of the Kingdom of Hawaii, and to offer an apology to Native Hawaiians on behalf of the United States for the overthrow of the Kingdom of Hawaii.

Whereas, prior to the arrival of the first Europeans in 1778, the Native Hawaiian people lived in a highly organized, self-sufficient, subsistent social system based on communal land tenure with a sophisticated language, culture, and religion;

Whereas, a unified monarchical government of the Hawaiian Islands the was established in 1810 under Kamehameha I, the first King of Hawaii;

Whereas, from 1826 until 1893, the United States recognized the independence of the Kingdom of Hawaii, extended full and complete diplomatic recognition to the Hawaiian Government, and entered into treaties and conventions with the Hawaiian monarchs to govern commerce and navigation in 1826, 1842, 1875 and 1887;

Whereas, the Congregational Church (now known as the United Church of Christ), through its American Board of Commissioners for Foreign Missions, sponsored and sent more than 100 missionaries to the Kingdom of Hawaii between 1820 and 1850;

Whereas, on January 14, 1893, John L. Stevens (hereafter referred to in this Resolution as the "United States Minister"), the United States Minister assigned to the sovereign and independent Kingdom of Hawaii conspired with a small group of non-Hawaiian residents of the Kingdom of Hawaii, including citizens of the United States, to overthrow the indigenous and lawful Government of Hawaii;

Whereas, in pursuance of the conspiracy to overthrow the Government of Hawaii, the United States Minister and the naval representatives of the United States caused armed naval forces of the United States to invade the sovereign Hawaiian nation on January 16, 1893, and to position themselves near the Hawaiian Government buildings and the Iolani Palace to intimidate Queen Lili'uokalani and her Government;

Whereas, on the afternoon of January 17,1893, a Committee of Safety that represented the American and European sugar planters, descendants of missionaries, and financiers deposed the Hawaiian monarchy and proclaimed the establishment of a Provisional Government;

Whereas, the United States Minister thereupon extended diplomatic recognition to the Provisional Government that was formed by the conspirators without the consent of the Native Hawaiian people or the lawful Government of Hawaii and in violation of treaties between the two nations and of international law;

Whereas, soon thereafter, when informed of the risk of bloodshed with resistance, Queen Lili'uokalani issued the following statement yielding her authority to the United States Government rather than to the Provisional Government:

"I Lili'uokalani, by the Grace of God and under the Constitution of the Hawaiian Kingdom, Queen, do hereby solemnly protest against any and all acts done against myself and the Constitutional Government of the Hawaiian Kingdom by certain persons claiming to have established a Provisional Government of and for this Kingdom.

"That I yield to the superior force of the United States of America whose Minister Plenipotentiary, His Excellency John L. Stevens, has caused United States troops to be landed on Honolulu and declared that he would support the Provisional Government.

"Now to avoid any collision of armed forces, and perhaps the loss of life, I do this under protest and impelled by said force yield my authority until such time as the Government of the United States shall, upon facts being presented to it, undo the action of its representatives and reinstate me in the authority which I claim as the Constitutional Sovereign of the Hawaiian Islands." Done at Honolulu this 17th day of January, A.D. 1893.

Whereas, without the active support and intervention by the United States diplomatic and military representatives, the insurrection against the Government of Queen Lili'uokalani would have failed for lack of popular support and insufficient arms;

Whereas, on February 1, 1893, the United States Minister raised the American flag and proclaimed Hawaii to be a protectorate of the United States;

Whereas, the report of a Residentially established investigation conducted by former Congressman James Blount into the events surrounding the insurrection and overthrow of January 17, 1893, concluded that the United States diplomatic and military representatives had abused their authority and were responsible for the change in government;

Whereas, as a result of this investigation, the United States Minister to Hawaii was recalled from his diplomatic post and the military commander of the United States armed forces stationed in Hawaii was disciplined and forced to resign his commission; Whereas, in a message to Congress on December 18, 1893, President Grover Cleveland reported accurately on the illegal acts of the conspirators, described such acts as an "act of war, committed with the participation of a diplomatic representative of the United States and without authority of Congress", and acknowledged that by such acts the government of a peaceful and friendly people was overthrown;

Whereas, President Cleveland further concluded that a "substantial wrong has thus been done which a due regard for our national character as well as the rights of the injured people requires we should endeavor to repair" and called for the restoration of the Hawaiian monarchy;

Whereas, the Provisional Government protested President Cleveland's call for the restoration of the monarchy and continued to hold state power and pursue annexation to the United States;

Whereas, the Provisional Government successfully lobbied the Committee on Foreign Relations of the Senate (hereafter referred to in this Resolution as the "Committee") to conduct a new investigation into the events surrounding the overthrow of the monarchy; annexation;

Whereas, the Committee and its chairman, Senator John Morgan, conducted hearings in Washington, D.C., from December 27, 1893, through February 26, 1894, in which members of the Provisional Government justified and condoned the actions of the United States Minister and recommended of Hawaii;

Whereas, although the Provisional Government was able to obscure the role of the United States in the illegal overthrow of the Hawaiian monarchy, it was unable to rally the support from two-thirds of the Senate needed to ratify a treaty of annexation;

Whereas, on July 4, 1894, the Provisional Government declared itself to be the Republic of Hawaii;

Whereas, on January 24, 1895, while imprisoned in Iolani Palace, Queen Lili'uokalani was forced by representatives of the Republic of Hawaii to officially abdicate her throne;

Whereas, in the 1896 United States Presidential election, William McKinley replaced Grover Cleveland;

Whereas, on July 7, 1898, as a consequence of the Spanish-American War, President McKinley signed the Newlands Joint Resolution that provided for the annexation of Hawaii;

Whereas, through the Newlands Resolution, the self-declared Republic of Hawaii ceded sovereignty over the Hawaiian Islands to the United States;

Whereas, the Republic of Hawaii also ceded 1,800,000 acres of crown, government and public lands of the Kingdom of Hawaii, without the consent of or compensation to the Native Hawaiian people of Hawaii or their sovereign government;

Whereas, the Congress, through the Newlands Resolution, ratified the cession, annexed Hawaii as part of the United States, and vested title to the lands in Hawaii to the United States;

Whereas, the Newlands Resolution also specified that treaties existing between Hawaii and foreign nations were to immediately cease and be replaced by United States treaties with such nations;

Whereas, the Newlands Resolution effected the transaction between the Republic of Hawaii and the United States Government;

Whereas, **the indigenous Hawaiian people never directly relinquished their claims to their inherent sovereignty as a people or over their national lands to the United States, either through their monarchy or through a plebiscite or referendum;**

Whereas, on April 30, 1900, President McKinley signed the Organic Act that provided a government for the territory of Hawaii and defined the political structure and powers of the newly established Territorial Government and its relationship to the United States;

Whereas, on August 21,1959, Hawaii became the 50th State of the United States;

Whereas, **the health and well-being of the Native Hawaiian people is intrinsically tied to their deep feelings and attachment to the land;**

Whereas, the long-range economic and social changes in Hawaii over the nineteenth and early twentieth centuries have been devastating to the population and to the health and well-being of the Hawaiian people;

Whereas, **the Native Hawaiian people are determined to preserve, develop and transmit to future generations their ancestral territory, and their cultural identity in accordance with their own spiritual and traditional beliefs, customs, practices, language, and social institutions;**

Whereas, in order to promote racial harmony and cultural understanding, the Legislature of the State of Hawaii has determined that the year 1993, should serve Hawaii as a year of special reflection on the rights and dignities of the Native Hawaiians in the Hawaiian and the American societies;

Whereas, **the Eighteenth General Synod of the United Church of Christ in recognition of the denomination's historical complicity in the illegal overthrow of the Kingdom of Hawaii in 1893 directed the Office of the President of the United Church of Christ to offer a public apology to the Native Hawaiian people and to initiate the process of reconciliation between the United Church of Christ and the Native Hawaiians;** and

Whereas, it is proper and timely for the Congress on the occasion of the impending one hundredth anniversary of the event, to acknowledge the historic significance of the illegal overthrow of the Kingdom of Hawaii, to express its deep regret to the Native Hawaiian people, and to support the reconciliation efforts of the State of Hawaii and the United Church of Christ with Native Hawaiians;

Now, therefore, be it Resolved by the Senate and House of Representatives of the United States of America in Congress assembled,

SECTION 1. ACKNOWLEDGMENT AND APOLOGY.

The Congress —

(1) on the occasion of the 100th anniversary of the illegal overthrow of the Kingdom of Hawaii on January 17, 1893, acknowledges

the historical significance of this event which resulted in the suppression of the inherent of Christ with Native Hawaiians sovereignty of the Native Hawaiian people;

(2) recognizes and commends efforts of reconciliation initiated by the State of Hawaii and the United Church;

(3) of the rights of Native Hawaiians to self-determination; APOLOGIZES TO NATIVE HAWAIIANS ON BEHALF OF THE PEOPLE OF THE UNITED STATES FOR THE OVERTHROW OF THE KINGDOM OF HAWAII ON JANUARY 17, 1893 WITH THE PARTICIPATION OF AGENTS AND CITIZENS OF THE UNITED STATES;

(4) expresses its commitment to acknowledge the ramifications of the overthrow of the Kingdom of Hawaii, in order to provide a proper foundation for reconciliation between the United States and the Native Hawaiian people; and

(5) urges the President of the United States to also acknowledge the ramifications of the overthrow of the Kingdom of Hawaii and to support reconciliation efforts between the United States and the Native Hawaiian people.

DEFINITIONS. As used in this Joint Resolution, the term "Native Hawaiians" means any individual who is a descendent of the aboriginal people who, prior to 1778, occupied and exercised sovereignty in the area that now constitutes the State of Hawaii.

DISCLAIMER. Nothing in this Joint Resolution is intended to serve as a settlement of any claims against the United States.—Approved November 23, 1993*

*(Bold face in Epilogue section added for emphasis and not in original document)

LILI'UOKALANI
Queen of the Hawaiian Islands

Statement of protest

"I Lili 'uokalani, by the Grace of God and under the Constitution of the Hawaiian Kingdom, Queen, do hereby solemnly protest against any and all acts done against myself and the constitutional government of the Hawaiian Kingdom by certain persons claiming to have established a provisional government of and for this Kingdom.

"That I yield to the superior force of the United States of America, whose minister plenipotentiary, His Excellence John L. Stevens, has caused United States' troops to be landed at Honolulu and declared that he would support the said provisional government.

"Now, to avoid any collision of armed forces and perhaps the loss of life, I do under this protest, and impelled by said force, yield my authority until such time as the Government of the United States shall, upon the facts being presented to it, undo the action of its representatives and reinstate me in the authority which I claim as the constitutional sovereign of the Hawaiian Islands."*

Voices of Maui

To review more recent
Voices of Maui
published since this first printing
read Lahaina News or
go to
voicesofmaui.com
Additional copies of this volume are available at amazon.com and leading retailers on Maui
(list on the web site)
A hui hou

Made in the USA
San Bernardino, CA
28 February 2014